LEARNING services

Cornwall College St Austell
Learning Centre – Level 5

This resource is to be returned on or before the last date stamped below. To renew items please contact the Centre

Three Week Loan

Kitchens and Bathrooms
Cuisines et Salles de Bain
Küchen und Bäder

Publishing Director • Directeur d'édition • Verlagsleitung
Nacho Asensio

Editor • Rédaction • Redaktion
Joana Furió

Documentation • Documentation • Dokumentation
Agnès Gallifa Hurtado

Design and Layout • Composition et maquette • Design und Layout
Núria Sordé Orpinell

Cover Design • Création de page de garde • Außengestaltung
Carlos Gamboa Permanyer

Translation • Traduction • Übersetzung
Bill Bain (English)
Elisabeth Bonjour Ruiz de Gopegui (Français)
Oliver Herzig (Deutsch)

Production • Production • Produktion
Juanjo Rodríguez Novel

Copyright © 2002 Atrium Group
Publishing project: Books Factory, S.L.
e-mail: books@booksfactory.org

Published by: Atrium Internacional de
México, S.A. de C.V.
Fresas 60 (Colonia del Valle)
03200 México D.F. MÉXICO

Telf: +525 575 90 94
Fax: +525 559 21 52
e-mail: atriumex@laneta.apc.org
www.atrium.com.mx

ISBN: 84-95692-07-4
National Book Catalogue Number:
B-34508-02

Printed in Spain
Grabasa, S.L.

Copyright © 2002 Atrium Group
Projet éditorial: Books Factory, S.L.
e-mail: books@booksfactory.org

Publié par: Atrium Internacional de
México, S.A. de C.V.
Fresas nº 60 (Colonia del Valle)
03200 México D.F. MÉXICO

Telf: +525 575 90 94
Fax: +525 559 21 52
e-mail: atriumex@laneta.apc.org
www.atrium.com.mx

ISBN: 84-95692-07-4
Dépôt légal : B-34508-02

Imprimé en France
Grabasa, S.L.

Copyright © 2002 Atrium Group
Verlagsprojekt Books Factory, S.L.
e-mail: books@booksfactory.org

Veröffentlicht durch: Atrium
Internacional de México, S.A. de C.V.
Fresas nº 60 (Colonia del Valle)
03200 México D.F. MÉXICO

Telef: +525 575 90 94
Fax: +525 559 21 52
e-mail: atriumex@laneta.apc.org
www.atrium.com.mx

ISBN: 84-95692-07-4
Gesetzliche Hinterlegung:
B-34508-02

Druck in Spanien
Grabasa, S.L.

Kitchens and Bathrooms
Cuisines et Salles de Bain
Küchen und Bäder

Kitchens
Contents

Cuisines
Index

Küchen
Inhaltsverzeichniss

Bathrooms

Contents

Salles de bain

Index

Bäder

Inhaltsverzeichniss

Introduction

The kitchen and the bathroom are the two rooms in the house that best transmit the spirit of an age. More than the living room or the bedrooms, where it is easy to wax sentimental and accumulate furniture, lamps, and paintings passed down from parents to children, the bathroom allows a greater scrutiny of our possessions in terms of function.

This is why, no matter how much the passage of time alternates the classical and the modern in setting the stage for our ideal home, it is undeniable that an objective view of the components of kitchens and baths reveals their degree of harmony with the times. And this is true not in the aesthetic sphere (we live in the century where anything goes), but in the social. Taking into account that both kitchen and bath are eminently practical spaces--associated with the ongoing nature of daily life and hygiene--we may pamper ourselves with technological advances and still indulge our love of dreaming of times past where things were done at a less demanding pace than in our own age. It might also be that our imaginations rise up into an ideal dimension in thoughts of the future, where the most undesirable tasks (by way of their routine nature) would be abolished and cease to be part of our obligations.

However, this is not the reason we might bid goodbye to the electric appliances that have contributed so much to our wellbeing, or to the hot water that allows us to keep up our corporal hygiene and the daily setting that is now synonymous with health.

Now that all these achievements are attainable goods for most of us, the innovation no longer consists in creating new gadgets that substitute manual tasks, but in refining their performance, conflating utility and beauty in a fusion where design assumes the role once played by a subdued artistry while technology handles the creation of new solutions--invisible or anodyne at first sight--to support these visions that comprise our ideal of life.

On the practical side, the aforementioned blend of beauty and technique may be glimpsed in our structuring of space. The kitchen, especially, serves as testing ground for all the advances in the field. Whether modern, rustic, designermade, or technological, the distribution of interior spaces will be a public challenge for our organizational skills. If electric appliances now take us into the world of electronics, shunning superfluous ornamentation and letting things practical monopolize the luxury role, the insides of closets and drawers renounce being relegated to the vacuum and to the disparaging generalization of the term catchall to take on the garb of a harmonizing mission from which emanates a proper hierarchy for each home. Where, objects occupy the place they should occupy according to how often they're put to use. Our eyes are wide open in admiration and desire when faced with the vision of these spice chests and vegetable boxes, with their specially laid out compartments for knives or even with electrical sockets to plug the appliances into. And this is without even speaking of the quality and the variety of the materials and the finishes employed, planned and calibrated down to the last detail to carry weights and hold sizes without spoiling the look of the overall project. The nooks and crannies have ceased to be associated with the cosmic "black hole" and taken on their fair share as guarantors of order: they include removable or swiveling shelves in modules planned as independ-

ent pieces. Many solutions in the internal closure or lighting systems of closets and dressers are the culmination of a large set of solutions that satisfy both the lover of classical urban style and the colorist post-modernist, reluctant to follow the herd.

The last two decades of the twentieth century left us the heritage of the body cult and concern with health as an individual responsibility. If the kitchen is aseptically organized like a laboratory where the healthiest menus are created, the bathroom ceases to be that disagreeable room our grandparents called the privy and becomes a sanctuary of wellbeing. No matter how much the furnishings and fittings take on one look or another, paying homage to the times that best reflect the ideals of their owners, it still becomes impossible to avoid the seduction of the new designs, especially when they offer a whole wide repertory of proposals whose wholesome virtues take us up to heights that verge on the sublime.

If the humble shower plate acquires qualities of excellence with materials that make it possible to create extra-flat surfaces as well as to make normative white redundant, the tubs (recessed, semi-detached or open) are doted with different shapes and colors. And with the mini-pools, additional devices make bathing, more than a sporadic pleasure, a spiritual experience to be repeated at will. Backrests, handles, and non-slip surfaces safeguard the user, massaged by controlled water turbulence, while the music that is piped in over the speaker available in some models transforms the bath into a music therapy session. Hydromassage cabins or saunas are also available, constituting an alternative for those who wish to take care of themselves but have less bathroom space.

The accessories and lighting also make up part of the concern for creating a space adequate to their use. The first ones manufactured were usually derived from the general style, although they took on a singular look thanks to the conceptual vigor of their design. In many cases, a simple hook, a faucet, a shelf combine with skilful grace and utility, transcending their specific original purpose and doubling as a small piece of sculpture. A correct lighting arrangement of spots combined with more general lights, will create an environment more in keeping with the style chosen for each room. Here, the choices range from the conventional look of a one-of model to the extravagance of an "authored" lamp. Thus, the search is always for features of a unique identity chosen from the best the market has to offer.

Style visualization and those components that best define our identity cannot avoid the reality of a series of unknowns (budget, surface area, distribution, family size...) without which we would not manage to bring the project our imagination so happily contemplates to its proper closure.

Introduction

Les cuisines et les salles de bain sont les pièces d'une maison qui transmettent le mieux l'esprit d'une époque, beaucoup plus que le salon ou les chambres à coucher, où, par sentiments, il est plus facile de conserver des meubles, des lampes et des tableaux hérités de pères en fils sans se poser de question sur leur utilité.

C'est pour cela que, malgré l'alternance du marché entre le classique et le moderne dans le but de créer le scénario idéal pour notre foyer, l'observation sans préjugés des différentes parties qui composent ces pièces essentielles dans notre vie, révélera notre degré d'harmonie avec le présent, non seulement du côté esthétique (c'est le siècle du « tous est permis ») mais aussi sociale. Comme la cuisine et la salle de bain son des espaces éminemment pratiques, associés à reproduire la vie et l'hygiène quotidiennes, il est impossible de ne pas profiter de tous les progrès technologiques existants même si nous adorons rêver du temps passé qui se déroulai à un rythme beaucoup moins exigent qu'à présent.

Il est bien possible, aussi, que notre imagination ai tendance à chercher une dimension idéale de future où les tâches les plus ingrates, si routinières soit elles, seront abolies et ne feront plus partie de nos obligations. Pourtant, l'idée d'oublier pour toujours les appareils électroménagers est inconcevable par le fait de leur grande utilité et du bien-être qu'ils nous apportent ; ni, non plus, l'eau chaude qui nous permet de maintenir l'hygiène de notre corps et de notre environnement, et qui est de ce fait synonyme de santé.

Depuis que tous ces biens peuvent être acquis par une grande majorité, la nouveauté n'est plus autant dans le fait de créer de nouveaux engins capables de remplacer les travaux réalisés manuellement, sinon plutôt d'améliorer les performances en conjuguant utilité et beauté, une fusion où d'une part le design assume le rôle tenu précédemment par l'artisanat traditionnelle pendant que la technologie se chargeait de présenter des solutions, invisibles ou anodines à première vue, pour renforcer cette vision des cho-   ses qui représentent notre idéal de vie.

Du côté pratique, on cédemment citée dans un laboratoire d'essai Autant si elle est monagement des espaces pacité d'organisation. Si tons à l'introduction permettre que les perrieur des placards et des du terme « four tous » nant d'une hiérarchie qui leur correspond sed'admiration et d'envie cons d'épices et de fédes prises de courant variété des matériaux et pour supporter poids et petits coins ne sont plus

aperçoit la conjonction de beauté et de technique préla structure de l'espace. La cuisine, surtout, est devenue pour toutes les avances obtenues dans ce domaine. derne, rustique, design ou de haute technologie, l'améinternes représentera un examen publique à notre caen matières d'appareils électroménagers nous assismassive d'une électronique qui fuit du superflue pour formances appartiennent au domaine du luxe, l'intétiroirs fuient du vide et de la généralisation méprisante pour assumer la mission de créer une harmonie émapropre à chaque foyer où les objets occupent la place lon la fréquence d'usage. Nous restons bouches bées devant ces éléments encastrés qui hébergent les flaculents, avec ses orifices pour les couteaux ou même pour petit appareils. Sans parler de la qualité et de La des finitions, travaillés et calibrés jusqu'au moindre détail dimensions sans endommager l'ensemble du projet. Les des « trous noirs cosmiques » et se chargent d'accomplir leurs fonctions de garants de l'ordre à travers l'installation d'étagères giratoires ou escamotables et devenant ainsi des objets créers comme des éléments indépendants. Les multiples solutions dans les systèmes de fermeture ou d'éclairage intérieur des placards et des vitrines aboutissent à une complète collection de succès qui satisfont autant les partisans du style urbain que post-moderne et coloriste, et qui fuient des règles établies.

Les deux dernières décennies du xx ème siècle nous ont laissé en héritage le culte du corps et la préoccupation pour la santé en tant que responsabilité individuelle. Si on organise sa cuisine avec l'hygiène d'un laboratoire pour créer les menus les plus sains, les salles de bain ne sont plus maintenant ces pièces ingrates à peine nommées par nos ancêtres, pour devenir un véritable sanctuaire pour le plaisir des sens.

Même si le mobilier et les sanitaires se déguisent d'un style ou d'un autre pour rendre hommage aux temps qui se conjuguent le mieux avec les idéaux de ses propriétaires, il est impossible de se soustraire à la séduction des nouveaux design, maximum quand ceux-ci nous offrent tout un répertoire de possibilités dont les vertus de salubrité nous élèvent à un niveau sublime.

Si une simple douche peut être qualifiée d'excellente par le fait d'être réalisée dans des matériaux qui permettent créer des superficies complètement plates tout en abandonnant la norme habituelle de la couleur blanche, les baignoires à leur tour (encastrables, sur pied ou indépendantes) présentent de multiples formes et coloris, où les mini piscines pleines de technologie secrètes convertissent le bain en une expérience spirituelle que l'ont peu répéter à volonté au lieu d'un simple plaisir occasionnel. Les dossiers, les accoudoirs et les fonds antiglisse veillent sur la sécurité de l'usager, massé par des tourbillons d'eau contrôlés, pendant que la musique jaillit du haut-parleur disponible dans certains modèles, tout en transformant le bain en une véritable session de musicothérapie. Dans un autre domaine, les cabines d'hydromassage ou de sauna représentent l'alternance pour ceux qui veulent augmenter leur capital santé mais ne disposent pas d'espace suffisant dans leur salle de bain. Les accessoires et l'éclairage sont aussi très importants au moment de créer l'ambiance idéale à leur fonction. Les premiers sont habituellement un dérivé du style général, bien qu'ils tendent à devenir plus singuliers grâce à la rigueur avec laquelle ils ont été crées. Dans certains cas, une simple crochet, un robinet ou une étagère conjuguent si positivement beauté et utilité qu'ils dépassent le stade du fonctionnel pour devenir une véritable petite sculpture. La correcte distribution de la lumière, divisée en éclairage générale et points de lumière permettra de créer l'environnement le plus en accord avec le style choisi pour chacune des pièces. Les différentes propositions vont ici du modèle le plus conventionnel à l'extravagance la plus totale d'une lampe « d'auteur » toujours à la recherche d'une identité personnelle entre ce qu'il y a de mieux dans le marché.

Naturellement, la simple observation du style et des caractéristiques qui traduisent le mieux notre propre identité ne peut en aucun cas éviter de s'en tenir à une série d'impondérables (devis, superficie, aménagement, membres de la famille etc...) sans lesquels il serai absolument impossible de mener à bien ce que notre imagination a anticipé avec tant de bonheur.

Einleitung

Küche und Bad sind die Räume der Wohnung, die den Geist einer Epoche am besten vermitteln; Mehr als Wohn- oder Schlafzimmer, in welchen sich normalerweise die Anwesenheit, der durch die Eltern vererbten Möbel, Lampen und Bilder, ohne diese in ihrer Funktion zu bewerten, verewigt.

Aufgrund dessen und obwohl sich für die Inszenierung unseres idealen Heimes im Laufe der Jahre klassisch und modern im Markt abwechseln, wird eine leidenschaftslose Beobachtung der Komponenten dieser wesentlichen Räume den Grad ihrer Harmonie mit dem Zeitgeist preisgeben, vielleicht nicht so sehr in ihrem ästhetischen Aspekt (wir befinden uns im Jahrhundert des "alles ist gültig") sondern eher im sozialen. Wenn man berücksichtigt, daß sowohl die Küche als auch das Bad ausergewöhnlich praktische Räume sind, veknüpft mit einer Nachbildung des täglichen Lebens bzw. der täglichen Hygiene, kann man es sich nicht leisten, dort auf irgendwelche technische Entwicklungen zu verzichten, auch wenn wir gerne von Zeiten, in welchen der Lebensrythmus weniger anspruchsvoll als der unsrige war, träumen. Es könnte auch sein, daß unsere Einbildung eine so ideale Dimension der Zukunft entwickelt, welche die lästigsten, weil routinehaften Arbeiten abschafft, so daß diese nicht mehr zu unseren täglichen Pflichten gehören würden. Trotzdem würden wir uns weder von den Elektrogeräten, welche soviel für unser Wohlbefinden getan haben, noch vom Warmwasser, welches die Körperhygiene und unsere Umweltrahmenbedingungen, die heutzutage gleichbedeutend mit unserem Gesundheitsstandart sind, ermöglicht, verabschieden wollen. Jetzt, da diese Errungenschaften für die Mehrheit erwerbbar sind, bestehen Neuerungen nicht mehr im Erfinden von Geräten, welche manuelle Arbeiten ersetzen, sondern die Leistung derselben so zu verfeinern, daß die Fusion von Nützlichkeit und Schönheit in einer Weise erreicht wird, die einerseits dem Design die Rolle des früher der Tradition untergeordneten Handwerks zuweißt, während andererseits die Technologie für auf den ersten Blick unsichtbare oder zumindest lindernde Lösungen zu sorgen hat, welche diese Vision, die unser Lebensideal bildet, unterstützen.

Unter dem praktischen Gesichtspunkt ahnt man die erwähnte Verbindung zwischen Schönheit und Nützlichkeit in der Strukturierung des Raumes. Vor allem die Küche wird zum Probefeld für sämtliche Fortschritte auf diesem Gebiet bestimmt. Gleichgültig ob modernes Design, rustikaler Stil oder neueste Technologie - die Aufteilung des internen Raums wird zur öffentlichen Prüfung unserer Organisationsfähigkeit. Wenn wir, was die Haushaltsgeräte betrifft, an der nachhaltigen Einführung der Elektronik teilnehmen, welche entbehrliche Dekoration vermeidet und die Leistungen derselben die Bezeichnung Luxus tragen lassen, sagt das Innere der Schränke und Schubladen sich vom Vakuum und der abwertenden Verallgemeinerung des Ausdrucks "Schneiderkästchen" los, um sich in einer harmonischen Mission wiederzufinden, aus der eine für jedes Heim eigenen Hirarchie hervorgeht und in welcher alle Gegenstände den je nach Häuffigkeit ihrer

rer Verwendung für sie geeigneten Platz finden werden. Unsere Augen werden sich bei dem Anblick dieser Schubladen mit Elementen, eingepasst für die Aufbewahrung von Gewürzglässchen und Hülsenfrüchte, mit Schlitzen für Messer und sogar mit Stromzuführungen für kleine Elektrogeräte, vor Bewunderung und Verlangen auf Tellergröße öffnen. Nicht zu vergessen ist die Qualität, die Vielfältigkeit der Materialien sowie die Verarbeitung, welche bis zum letzten Detail so ausgedacht und kalibriert ist, daß sie die Gewichte und Größen aushält ohne die gesamte Einheit zu ruinieren. Die früher nutzlosen Winkel gleichen nicht mehr kosmischen "schwarzen Löchern", sondern erfüllen ihren Part, in dem sie

Ordnung durch die Aufnahme von herausnehmbaren oder drehba-
ren, als unabhängige Teile ausgedachten Regalbrettern schaffen.
Vielfältige Lösungen bei den internen Beleuchtungs- und Schließsystemen der Schränke und
Glasvitrinen runden eine lange Reihe von Erfolgen, die sowohl die Freunde des post-modernen und
bunten Stils, welche den etablierten Regeln nur ungern folgen, als auch die Liebhaber des klassischen und urbanen Stils zufrieden stellen, ab.
Die letzten zwei Jahrzehnte dieses Jahrhunderts haben uns als Erbschaft den Körperkult sowie die
Sorge um die Gesundheit als eine persönliche Verantwortung hinterlassen. So wie die Küche mit der
Keimfreiheit eines Labors, in welchem die gesündesten Menus vorbereitet werden, gestaltet wird, ist
auch das Bad nicht mehr jener hässliche Teil der Wohnung, den unsere Großeltern noch "Abort"
nannten, sondern zu einem Tempel des Wohlbefindens mutiert. Gleichgültig wie stark die Möbel
oder sanitären Einrichtungen sich dem Stil der Zeit ihrer Besitzer anpassen: Es ist unmöglich sich den
Verlockungen der neuen Entwürfe zu entziehen, besonders wenn diese uns ein Repertoire von
Vorschlägen anbieten, welche in ihren gesundheitlichen Eigenschaften an der Grenze zum
Verherrlichenden gipfeln. Wenn schon die bescheidene Dusche so ausgezeichnete Eigenschaften,
wie die Schaffung von extraglatten Oberflächen, erlangt und sich noch dazu von weiß als
maßgebender Farbe verabschiedet, dann verwandeln Badewannen (eingebaute genauso wie freistehende, und angebaute) durch multiple Formen und Farben, und
Minischwimmbäder mit verborgenen Erfindungsgaben, das Baden nicht mehr zu einem
gelegentlichen Genuß, sondern vielmehr zu einer nach belieben wiederholbaren, spiri-
tuellen Erfahrung. Lehnen, Griffe und rutschfeste Böden bewachen die physische
Sicherheit des Benutzers, welcher durch kontrolliert turbulente Gewässer massiert wird, während
die in einigen Modelen verfügbaren Lautsprecher durch ihre Musik das Baden in eine
Musiktherapiesitzung verwandeln.
Bei anderer Gewichtung der Genüsse bilden Unterwassermassagekabinen oder die Sauna die
Alternativen für diejenigen, welche sich pflegen möchten, aber über einen eingeschränkteren
Platzspielraum verfügen.
Zubehörteile und Beleuchtung sind ebenfalls Part des Gedankens, eine ihrer Funktion angemessene
Ambiente zu schaffen. Erstere sind normalerweise eine Folge des Gesamtstils, obwohl sie auch durch
ihre konzeptuelle Strenge mit der sie erarbeitet wurden, eigenständig sein können. In vielen Fällen
kombinieren ein einfacher Haken, Armaturen oder auch ein Regal, Anmutigkeit und Nützlichkeit so
treffsicher, daß ihre eigentliche Funktion von der Vornehmheit einer kleinen Skulptur geprägt wird.
Eine korrekte Anordnung des Lichts, aufgeteilt in direkte und indirekte Beleuchtung, wird für jedes
Einzelstück das adäquateste Umfeld in dem für ihn gewählten Stil schaffen. Hier gehen die
Angebote vom Konventionalismus eines Serienmodels bis zur Extravaganz einer
"Schriftstellerlampe", somit immer auf der Suche nach eigenen Identitätsmerkmalen und innerhalb
des Besten was der Markt uns anzubieten hat.
Selbstverständlich kann dieser Stil mit seinen Komponenten, welcher unsere eigene
Identität am Besten übersetzt, sich nicht von einigen Unwägbarkeiten (vorhandene finan-
zielle Mittel, Raumangebot, Logistik, Familienmitglieder,...) befreien, ohne welche wir aller-
dings unfähig wären unser, in unserer Vorstellungskraft bereits vorweggenommenes,
Projekt gelungen abzuschließen.

Kitchens

Cuisines

Küchen

Modern / *Les modernes*
Moderne

The modern style exploits all things new and makes them its own, allowing convenient reformulation of what has been achieved by previous styles. The free combination of materials, colors, heights, and lines breaks the monotony of the modular structure to allow a pleasant transition in open kitchens to the other rooms of the house.

Le style moderne profite de toutes les nouveautés et se permet de profiter selon sa convenance des styles du passé. Le fait de combiner librement matériaux, coloris, hauteur et lignes romps avec la monotonie de la structure modulaire, permettant ainsi une transition agréable dans les cuisines qui s'ouvrent vers les autres pièces de la maison.

Der moderne Stil nützt und macht sich sämtliche Neuerungen zu eigen und erlaubt sich die Beiträge der vorausgegangenen Stile zu seinem Nutzen umzuformulieren. Die freie Kombination von Materialien, Farben Höhen und Linien räumt mit der Monotonie der Modulstruktur auf und erlaubt angenehme Übergänge zwischen offenen Küchen und anderen Räumen des Hauses.

Previous page:
Nobilia Pia Mod.

Page précédente:
Mod. Pia de chez Nobilia.

Auf der vorherigen Seite:
Modell Pia von Nobilia.

Range in a Casawell base cabinet.

Cuisine avec un seul front
de chez Casawell.

Küche in einer Front von Casawell.

Nolte Avant Mod.

Mod. Avant de chez Nolte.

Modell Avant von Nolte.

Tielsa kitchen island.

*Cuisine avec île de
travail de chez Tielsa.*

Küche mit Arbeitsinsel
von Tielsa.

Nolte Como Mod.

Mod. Como de chez Nolte.

Modell Como von Nolte.

Nolte Star 271 Mod.

Mod. Star 271 de chez Nolte.

Modell Star 271 von Nolte.

Alno L-shaped kitchen.

*Cuisine avec île de travail
de chez Alno.*

Küche mit Arbeitsinsel
von Alno.

Alno small L-shaped kitchen.

Cuisine en forme de L de chez Alno.

Küche in L-Form von Alno.

Nolte Ravenna Mod.   *Mod. Ravenna*   Modell Ravenna
                       de chez Nolte.   von Nolte.

Nolte Star 274 Mod.

Mod. Star 274
de chez Nolte.

Modell Star 274
von Nolte.

Nolte Verona Mod.   *Mod. Verona de chez Nolte.*   **Modell Verona von Nolte.**

Nolte Roma Mod.

Mod. Roma de chez Nolte.

Modell Roma von Nolte.

Nobilia Gala Mod.

Mod. Gala de chez Nobilia.

Modell Gala von Nobilia.

Nolte L-shaped kitchen.

Cuisine en forme de L de chez Nolte.

Küche in L-Forum von Nolte.

Nobilia Cortina Mod.

Mod. Cortina de chez Nobilia.

Modell Cortina von Nobilia.

Nobilia Colorado Mod.

Mod. Colorado de chez Nobilia.

Modell Colorado von Nobilia.

Mod. Cento de Nobilia.

Mod. Cento de chez Nobilia.

Modell Cento von Nobilia.

Nobilia Rondo Mod.

Mod. Rondo de chez Nobilia.

Modell Rondo von Nobilia.

Nobilia Fontana Mod.

Mod. Fontana de chez Nobilia.

Modell Fontana von Nobilia.

An Allmilmo
classic model.

*Un modèle classique
de Chez Allmilmo.*

Ein klassisches Modell
von Allmilmo.

Alno kitchen-living room.

Cuisine-salon de chez Alno.

Wohnzimmerküche
von Alno.

Febal Lemon Mod.

Mod. Lemon de chez Febal.

Modell Lemon von Febal.

Nobilia Morena Mod.

Mod. Morena de chez Nobilia.

Modell Morena von Nobilia.

Febal Mixer Mod.

*Mod. Mixer
de chez Febal.*

Modell Mixer
von Febal.

Next page:
Nobilia Natura Mod.

*Page suivante:
Mod. Natura de chez Nobilia.*

Auf der folgenden Seite:
Modell Natura con Nobilia.

Next page:
Nobilia Orion Mod.

Page suivante:
Mod. Orion
de chez Nobilia.

Auf der folgenden Seite
Modell Orion
von Nobilia.

Nolte Ravenna Mod.   *Mod. Ravenna de chez Nolte.*   Modell Ravenna von Nolte.

Nobilia Natura Mod.

Mod. Natura de chez Nobilia.

Modell Natura von Nobilia.

Allmilmo L-shaped kitchen.

Cuisine en forme de L de chez Allmilmo.

Küche in L-Form von Allmilmo.

Kitchen with one front by Allmilmo.

Cuisine avec un seul front de chez Allmilmo.

Küche in einer Front von Allmilmo.

Nobilia Tivoli Mod.   *Mod. Tivoli de chez Nobilia.*   Modell Tivoli von Nobilia.

Alno L-shaped kitchen.

Cuisine en forme de L de chez Alno.

Küche in L-Form von Alno.

Detail of Alno kitchen.

Détail d'une cuisine de chez Alno.

Detailansicht einer Alnoküche.

Nolte Life Mod.

Mod. Life de chez Nolte.

Modell Life von Nolte.

Alno low modules.

*Cuisine avec ligne
d'éléments bas de chez Alno.*

**Küche in Niedrigmodulen
Alno.**

Alno L-shaped kitchen.

Cuisine en forme de L de chez Alno.

Küche in L-Form von Alno.

Alno slide-in range and work island.

Cuisine avec un seul front et île centrale de travail de chez Alno.

Küche in einer Front mit Arbeitsinsel von Alno.

Nobilia Lago Mod.

Mod. Lago de chez Nobilia.

Modell Lago von Nobilia.

Febal Sally Mod.

Mod. Sally de chez Febal.

Modell Sally von Febal.

Nolte Lido Mod.

Mod. Lido de chez Nolte.

Modell Lido von Nolte.

Nolte Milano Mod.

Mod. Milano de chez Nolte.

Modell Milano von Nolte.

Allmilmo Ponte Mod.

Mod. Ponte de chez Allmilmo.

Modell Ponte von Allmilmo.

Febal Orange Mod.

Mod. Orange de chez Febal.

Modell Orange von Febal.

Next page: kitchen with work island and sink.

Page suivante: Cuisine avec île centrale de lavage de chez Alno.

Auf der folgenden Seite: Küche mit Waschinsel von Alno.

Casawell open kitchen.

Cuisine ouverte de chez Casawell.

Offene Küche von Casawell.

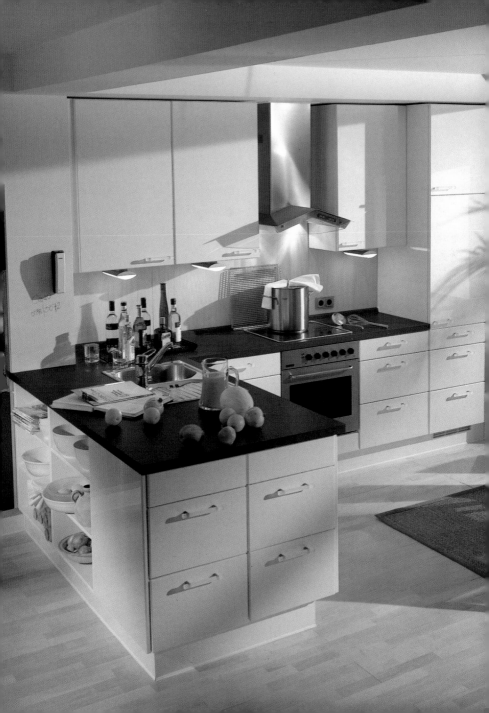

Nolte Verona 235 Mod.

Mod. Verona 235 de chez Nolte.

Modell Verona 235 von Nolte.

Alno cabinets and
slide-in range.

*Cuisine avec deux
fronts de chez Alno.*

Küche mit zwei
Fronten von Alno.

Detail of Casawell
kitchen.

*Détail d'une cuisine
de chez Casawell.*

Detailansicht einer
Casawellküche.

Febal Playa 01 Mod.

Mod. Playa 01 de chez Febal.

Modell Playa 01 von Febal.

Next page:
Febal Playa 15 Mod.

Page suivante:
Mod. Playa 15 de chez Febal.

Auf der folgenden Seite:
Modell Playa 15 von Febal.

Febal Playa 08 Mod.

Mod. Playa 08 de chez Febal.

Modell Playa 08 von Febal.

Leicht L-shaped kitchen.

Cuisine en forme de L de chez Leicht.

Küche in L-Form von Leicht.

Three Alno cabinet units.

Cuisine avec trois fronts de chez Alno.

Küche mit drei Fronten von Alno.

Alno kitchen.   *Cuisine en forme de L de chez Alno.*   **Küche mit zwei Fronten von Alno.**

Alno cabinets on legs. *Cuisine sur pattes de chez* Küche auf FüBen
Alno. von Alno.

An Alno classic model.

Un modèle classique de chez Alno.

Ein klassisches Modell von Alno.

Detail of slide-in range of preceding model.

Détail du plan de cuisson de la précédente.

Detailansicht der Kochfront des vorherigen Modells.

Alno kitchen with
central work island.

*Cuisine avec île centrale
de chez Alno.*

**Küche mit zentraler
Insel von Alno.**

Florida Venus Mod.

Mod. Venus de chez Florida.

Modell Venus von Florida.

Nobilia Star 278 Mod.

*Mod. Star 278
de chez Nobilia.*

Modell Star 278
von Nobilia.

Alno kitchen with units
of various heights.

*Cuisine de différents
niveaux de chez Alno.*

Küche mit in Höhe
verschiedenen Elementen
von Alno.

Nolte Lido 435 Mod. *Mod. Lido 435 de chez Nolte.* Modell Lido 435 von Nolte.

Alno L-shaped kitchen.

Cuisine en forme de L de chez Alno.

Three cabinet units by Leicht.

Cuisine avec trois plans de travail de chez Leicht.

Küche mit drei Fronten von Leicht.

Küche in L-Form von Alno.

Martinica cleaning
module.

*Élément de lavage
de chez Martinica.*

Reinigungsmodul
von Martinica.

Martinica slide-in range.

*Cuisine avec un seul front
de chez Martinica.*

Küche in einer Front
von Martinica.

Martinica dining
room table.

*Table à repas de chez
Martinica.*

Esstisch von Martinica.

Martinica L-shaped
kitchen with table.

*Cuisine en forme de L
avec table à repas de
chez Martinica.*

Küche in L-Form mit
Tisch von Martinica.

Detail of extractor hood by Martinica.

*Détail d'une hotte extracteur
de chez Martinica.*

Detailansicht des Dunstabzugs
von Martinica.

Florida Trendy Mod.

Mod. Trendy de chez Florida.

Modell Trendy von Florida.

Next page:
Florida extractable
Trendy Mod. Table.

Page suivante:
Table escamotable du mod.
Trendy de chez Florida.

Auf der nächsten Seite:
Ausziehbarer Tisch des
Modells Trendy von Florida.

Florida Mixer
2000 Mod.

Mod. Mixer 2000
di Florida.

Modell Mixer
2000 von Florida.

Leicht L-shaped
kitchen.

*Cuisine en forme de
L de chez Leicht.*

Küche in L-Form
von Leicht.

Leicht kitchen with cooking
annex.

*Cuisine en forme de L de chez
Leicht.*

Küche mit Kochhalbinsel
von Leicht.

Mobalpa kitchen with
cooking island.

*Cuisine avec île
de cuisson de chez
Mobalpa.*

Küche mit Kochinsel
von Mobalpa.

Leicht model
base cabinets.

*Cuisine avec trois plans
de travail de chez Leicht.*

Küche mit drei Fronten
von Leicht.

Different combinations
of Siematic units.

*Cuisine avec plusieurs
plans de travail
de chez Siematic.*

Küche mit verschiedenen
Fronten von Siematic.

Two Siematic cabinet
units.

*Cuisine avec deux plans
de travail de chez
Siematic.*

Küche mit 2 Fronten
von Siematic.

Nolte apartment modules. *Éléments pour studio de chez Nolte.* **Module für Apartments von Nolte.** Nolte Avant 470 Mod.

Mod. Avant 470 de chez Nolte.

Modell Avant 470 von Nolte.

Mobalpa Sarila Brat Mod.

Mod. Brat de chez Mobalpa Sarila.

Modell Brat von Mobalpa Sarila.

Nolte kitchen with dining room annex.	*Cuisine avec salle à manger annexés de chez Nolte.*	Küche mit zusätzlichem Essbereich von Nolte.

Mobalpa L-shaped kitchen.   *Cuisine en forme de L de chez Mobalpa.*   Küche in L-Form von Mobalpa.

Mobalpa kitchen with cooking island.

Cuisine avec île de cuisson de chez Mobalpa.

Küche mit Kochinsel von Mobalpa.

Nolte Flair Mod.   *Mod. Flair de chez Nolte.*   **Modell Flair von Nolte.**

Nolte Linea Mod.

Mod. Linea de chez Nolte.

Modell Linea von Nolte.

Nolte Star 27 Mod.

*Mod. Star 27
de chez Nolte.*

Modell Star 27
von Nolte.

Nolte Relief Mod.

Mod. Relief de chez Nolte.

Modell Relief von Nolte.

Detail of
Mobalpa kitchen   *Plan de cuisson
de chez Mobalpa.*   Kochfront
von Mobalpa.

Mobalpa Ora 40601 Mod.

*Mod. Ora 40601
de chez Mobalpa.*

Modell Ora 40601
von Mobalpa.

Next page:
Mobalpa Ora 40604 Mod.

*Page suivante :
Mod. Ora 40604
de chez Mobalpa.*

Auf der folgenden Seite:
Modell Ora 40604
von Mobalpa.

Mobalpa PVL Mod.

Mod. PVL de chez Mobalpa.

Modell PVL von Mobalpa.

Nobilia Pia Mod.

Mod. Pia de chez Nobilia.

Modell Pia von Nobilia.

Casawell module with
shelves.

*Élément avec étagères
de chez Casawell.*

Modul mit Regalen
von Casawell.

Febal Onda Mod.

Mod. Onda de chez Febal.

Modell Onda von Febal.

Islands

The work island organizes a part of the cooking tasks, acting as a distributor to different fronts. Modern technology allows installation of cooktops into the island, and even refrigerators. But the free space in the base is distributed among drawers, cabinets, and shelf space. A derivation of this concept is the peninsula, which has also been freed to allow any of the essential kitchen functions, including counter meals.

Les îles

Les îles de travail possèdent une partie des fonctions culinaires en agissant comme distributeur vers les différents plans de travail. La technologie la plus moderne permet d'y installer une plaque de cuisson ou un évier, et de profiter des espaces libres restants pour y placer des tiroirs, des placards, ou des étagères. Il existe aussi une variété nommée presqu'île, qui, une foi libérée des idées préconçues est prête à accueillir n'importe quelle fonction y compris celle de servir de barre pour manger.

Inseln

Die Arbeitsinsel verknüpft einen Teil der kulinarischen Arbeiten in Verteilfunktion mit den verschieden Fronten der Küche. Die moderne Technologie erlaubt in ihnen die Installation von Kochplatten und sogar von Spülen, während im freien Raum des Unterbaus Schubladen, Schränke und Hohlräume für Regale verteilt werden. Eine Ableitung ist die Halbinsel, welche sich auch vom Klischee befreit hat und sich darauf vorbereitet, die unerlässlichen Funktionen inklusive des Esstresens in sich aufzunehmen.

Previous page:
Siematic kitchen island.

Page précédente:
Île centrale de travail
de chez Siematic.

Auf der vorherigen Seite:
Arbeitsinsel von Siematic.

Febal Flipper 1 Mod.

Mod. Flipperl de chez Febal.

Modell Flipper 1 von Febal.

Nolte Delta 764 Mod.

Mod. Delta 764 de chez Nolte.

Modell Delta 764 von Nolte.

Allmilmo Ponte 02 Mod.

*Mod. Ponte 02
de chez Allmilmo.*

Modell Ponte 02
von Allmilmo.

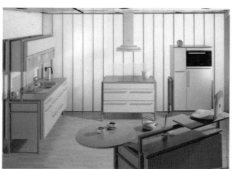

Tielsa kitchen with
work island.

*Cuisine avec île centrale
de travail de chez Tielsa.*

Küche mit
Arbeitsinsel von Tielsa.

Two Tielsa cabinet units with dining room work island.

Cuisine avec deux fronts et île centrale de travail- table à repas de chez Tielsa.

Küche mit zwei Fronten, Arbeitsinsel und Essbereich von Tielsa.

Tielsa kitchen with central work island.

Cuisine avec île centrale de travail centrale de chez Tielsa.

Küche mit zentraler Arbeitsinsel von Tielsa.

Alno kitchen with work cooktop incorporated in work island.

Cuisine avec éléments vitrine de chez Tielsa.

Küche mit Vitrinenelement von Tielsa.

Alno kitchen with
work cooktop
incorporated in work
island.

*Cuisine avec un seul
front et île centrale de
cuisson de chez Alno.*

Küche mit
Kochinsel von Alno.

Alno cabinet units and
cooktop island.

*Cuisine avec île centrale
de cuisson de chez Alno.*

Küche in einer Front mit
Kochinsel von Alno.

Febal Onda 05 Mod.   *Mod. Onda 05 de chez Febal.*   Modell Onda 05 von Febal.

Alno cabinet units   *Cuisine avec deux*   Kütche mit zwei
and cooktop island.   *fronts de chez Alno.*   Fronten von Alno.

Siematic professional
style kitchen.

*Cuisine de style
professionnel
de chez Siematic.*

Küche im professionellen
Stil von Siematic.

Febal work island and
fitted cabinets.

*Île centrale avec éléments
encastrés de chez Febal.*

Arbeitsinsel und
eingebaute Module von
Febal.

Allmilmo Ponte 01 Mod.

Mod. Ponte 01 de Allmilmo.

Modell Ponte 01 von Allmilmo.

Nolte Lido 438 Mod.

Mod. Lido 438 de chez Nolte.

Modell Lido 438 von Nolte.

Two Miele cabinet units with
central kitchen island.

*Cuisine avec deux fronts et île
centrale de chez Miele.*

Küche mit zwei Fronten und
zentraler Insel von Miele.

Miele Blue Mod.

Mod. Blue de chez Miele.

Modell Blue von Miele.

Next page:
Poggen professional
kitchen.

Page suivante:
Cuisine professionnelle
de chez Poggen.

Auf der nächsten Seite:
Professionelle Küche
von Poggen.

Designer kitchens / *Les Design Designer*

The designer kitchen impacts visually and provides high functionality while relegating forms to their structural value of distributing the basic cooking tasks. The interplay between revealing and concealing and the use of new materials in surfaces and electrical appliances make the designer kitchen recommendable for homes where space, whether abundant or minimal, calls for combined uses. Steel, synthetics, and striking colors are the hallmarks of this style, which fluctuates between solemnity and irony.

Les cuisines de design parient principalement sur l' impacte visuel et la fonctionnalité, et la forme devient une simple valeur structurelle :distribuer les devoirs principaux de l'art de cuisiner. C'est le style le plus recommandé pour tous ces logis où l'espace, autant par excès comme par défaut, nous obligent à créer un hybride de différentes fonctions, grâce à son jeu entre l'exhibition et la discrétion, ainsi qu'à l'apport de nouveaux matériaux appliqués aux différentes superficies et appareils d'électroménagers. L'acier, des surfaces synthétiques et des couleurs surprenantes constituent le label qui définit un style qui fluctue entre la solennité et l'ironie.

Die Designerküche setzt auf die visuelle Wirkung und die Funktionalität, während sie die Formen in ihren strukturellen Wert verbannt: das sich Aufteilen der Grundarbeiten der kulinarischen Arbeit. Das Spiel zwischen Zurschaustellung und Verschleierung gemeinsam mit dem Beitrag neuer Materialien für Oberflächen und Elektrogeräte machen diese für Wohnungen in welchen die Platzmöglichkeiten, sei es durch Übermaß oder durch Mangel, zur Hybridisierung der Funktionen zwingen, empfehlenswert. Stahl, synthetische Oberflächen und ungewöhnliche Farben bilden das Unterscheidungsmerkmal eines Stils der zwischen erhabenem Ernst und Ironie schwankt.

Previous page:
Aluminium kitchen by Schiffini.

*Page precedente:
Cuisine avec partie frontale en d'aluminium de chez Schiffini.*

Auf der vorherigen Seite:
Küche mit Aluminiumfront von Schiffini.

U-shaped kitchen by Schiffini.

Cuisine avec trois fronts de chez Schiffini.

Küche mit drei Fronten von Schiffini.

Strato L-shaped kitchen with cooking island.

Cuisine en forme de L avec île centrale de cuisson de chez Strato.

Küche in L-Form mit Kochinsel von Strato.

Schiffini range and dishwasher module.

Élement de cuisson et lavage de chez Schiffini.

Koch- und Waschmodul von Schiffini.

Previous page:
washing machine
cabinet with synthetic
counter American
kitchen.

Page précédente:
Espace lavage sur un plan
de travail synthétique.

Auf der vorherigen Seite:
Waschfront mit
syntetischer Arbeitsfläche.

Nolte Ad. Mode-Namay Mod.

Kitchnette mod. Ad.
Mode-Namay de chez Nolte.

Wohnküche modell Ad.
Mode-Namay von Nolte.

American kitchen.

Kitchnette.

Wohnküche.

Allmilmo L-shaped kitchen
with central island.

*Cuisine en forme de L avec île
centrale de chez Allmilmo.*

Küche in L-Form mit
zentraler Insel von Allmilmo.

Mobalpa Sarila
Libera Mod.

*Mod. Libera de chez
Mobalpa Sarila.*

Modell Libera von
Mobalpa Sarila.

Alsa kitchen with sink
incorporated in work island.

*Cuisine avec île centrale
de lavage de chez Alsa.*

Küche mit Waschinsel
von Alsa.

Alsa cabinets on three,
walls with cooktop in
kitchen island.

*Cuisine avec trois fronts
et île centrale de cuisson
de chez Alsa.*

Küche mit drei Fronten
und Kochinsel von Alsa.

Poggen L-shaped kitchen with
cooktop in work island.

*Cuisine en forme de L avec île centrale
de cuisson de chez Poggen.*

Küche in L-Form mit Kochinsel
von Poggen.

Alno cabinets on two walls.

Cuisine avec deux fronts de chez Alno.

Küche mit zwei Fronten von Alno.

Previous page:
Miele loft kitchen.

Page précédente :
Cuisine pour loft
de chez Miele.

Auf der vorherigen Seite:
Küche für Lofts
von Miele.

Siemens slide-in range
and cabinets.

Cuisine avec un front
de chez Siemens.

Küche in einer Front
von Siemens.

Alno L-shaped kitchen.

*Cuisine en forme de L
de chez Alno.*

Küche in L-Form
von Alno.

Giamaica L-shaped kitchen
with work island annex.

*Cuisine en forme de L avec île
annexée de chez Giamaica.*

Küche in L-Form mit
zusätzlicher Insel
von Giamaica.

Alno fitted kitchen with
breakfast counter.

*Cuisine encastrée avec île
centrale de travail- table
à repas de chez Alno.*

Einbauküche mit
Essinsel von Alno.

Leicht kitchen with cooktop
island.

*Cuisine avec île de cuisson
adossée de chez Leicht.*

Küche mit angebauter
Kochinsel von Leicht.

Leicht L-shaped kitchen
with dining room.

*Cuisine en forme de L de
chez Leicht.*

Küche in L-Form, mit
Esszimmer von Leicht.

106

Mobalpa L-shaped
kitchen with display-case
module.

*Cuisine en forme de L
avec élément vitrine
de chez Mobalpa.*

Küche in L-Form mit
Vitrinenmodul
von Mobalpa.

Elledue-House cabinets
with semi-freestanding
cooktop.

*Cuisine avec deux fronts
et île de cuisson adossée
de chez Elledue-House.*

Küche mit zwei Fronten
und angebautenr Kochinsel
von Elledue-House.

Siematic cabinets.

*Cuisine avec deux fronts de
chez Siematic.*

Küche mit zwei Fronten
von Siematic.

Mobalpa-Sarila Familia
38 Mod.

*Mod. Familia 38 de chez
Mobalpa-Sarila.*

Modell Familia 38 von
Mobalpa-Sarila.

Febal Joker 01 Mod.

Mod. Joker 01 de chez Febal.

Modell Joker 01 von Febal.

Mobalpa-Sarila
Familia 1 Mod.

*Mod. Familia 1 de chez
Mobalpa-Sarila.*

Modell Familia 1 von
Mobalpa-Sarila.

Febal Joker 05 Mod.

Mod. Joker 05 de chez Febal.

Modell Joker 05 von Febal.

Mobalpa-Sarila professional
style kitchen.

*Cuisine de style
professionnel de chez
Mobalpa- Sarila.*

Küche im professionellen
Stil von Mobalpa-Sarila.

Febal Sally Mod.

Mod. Sally de chez Febal.

Modell Sally von Febal.

Nobilia Techno Mod.

*Mod. Techno
de chez Nobilia.*

Modell Techno
von Nobilia.

Mobalpa-Sarila
Noumero Mod.

*Mod. Noumero de chez
Mobalpa-Sarila.*

Modell Noumero von
Mobalpa-Sarila.

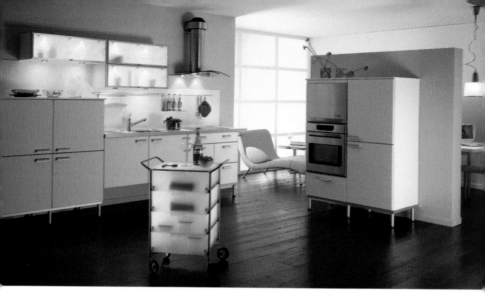

Mobalpa apartment
kitchen.

*Cuisine pour studio
de chez Mobalpa.*

**Küche für Appartments
von Mobalpa.**

Poggen professional
style kitchen.

*Cuisine de style
professionnel
de chez Poggen.*

**Küche im professionellen
Stil von Poggen.**

Previous page:
Poggen two-tone kitchen
with work island.

Page précédente:
Mod. Fue de chez Poggen.

Auf der vorherigen Seite:
Modell Fue von Poggen.

Detail of Poggen kitchen.

Détail d'un plan de cuisson
de chez Poggen.

Detailansicht einer Kochinsel
von Poggen.

Previous page:
Poggen two-tone kitchen
with work island.

Page suivante:
Cuisine bicolore avec
île centrale de travail
de chez Poggen.

Auf der folgenden Seite:
Zweifarbige Küche
mit Arbeitsinsel
von Poggen.

Classical / *Les classique et les rustiques* Klassische/Rustikale

The favorite style of the real homebodies keeps its preference for finishings in wood and other natural materials. It also favors solemn or regal colors, without giving up the innovative, always subject to use-orientation and uncompromising on ornamental detail: pilasters, cornices, latticed doors, wainscoting, and extractor hoods. The dinner tables and the work islands also blend in no matter whether they are found in the rural mansion or the humble apartment so coveted these days.

C'est le style préféré des personnes les plus familiales parce qu'il maintient l'amour pour le bois et les matériaux naturels, ainsi que les couleurs solennelles et majestueuses, sans pour autant renier du progrès et toujours attaché à une fonctionnalité qui ne prend jamais le dessus sur les éléments décoratifs : des colonnades, des corniches, des grillages, des panneaux en relief et des hottes-extracteur en maçonnerie. Les tables à repas et les îles centrales de travail se conjuguent également dans les grandes maisons de maître et dans les simples maisons de campagne, si en vogue actuellement.

Der vom häuslichen Menschen favorisierte Stil bleibt bei seiner Zuneigung für Ausfertigungen in Holz, natürlichen Materialien, sowie für ernste oder erhabene Farben, ohne jedoch Neuerungen, die von der Funktionalität behewscht werden und welche nicht den dekorativen Details wie zum Beispiel Pilaster, Gesimsverzierungen, Jalousien, Reliefpaneele oder Dunstabzügen die Geltung rauben, zu verneinen. Esstische und Arbeitsinseln, sowohl solche die sich auf Landhausmodele beziehen als auch die in der heutigen Zeit so geschätzten einfachen Hausfrauenmodele, setzen auch auf das Zusammenspiel.

Previous page:
Alno kitchen with work island

Page précédente:
Cuisine avec île centrale de travail
de chez Alno.

Auf der vorherigen Seite:
Küche mit Arbeitsinsel von Alno.

Alno cabinetry on three walls
with center island.

Cuisine avec trois fronts et île
centrale de chez Alno.

Küche mit drei Fronten und
zentraler Insel von Alno.

Elledue Stilnovo model
L-shaped kitchen.

Cuisine en forme de L de
chez Stilnovo de Elledue.

Küche in L-Form
Stilnovo von Elledue.

Detail of Elledue Prestige sink.

Détail de l'espace lavage Prestige
de chez Elledue.

Detailansicht des Waschbereichs
Prestige von Elledue.

Slide-in range
(Elledue Prestige).

*Détail de l'espace de cuisson
Prestige de chez Elledue.*

Detailansicht des
Kochbereichs Prestige
von Elledue.

Detail of Elledue Prestige
kitchen.

*Détail d'une cuisine
Prestige de chez Elledue.*

Detailansicht einer
Küche Prestige von
Elledue.

Dinner table with drawers
(Elledue Prestige).

*Table à repas avec tiroirs
Prestige de chez Elledue.*

Esstisch mit Schubladen
Prestige von Elledue.

Detail of cabinet units
(Elledue Prestige).

*Détail d'un front de cuisine
Prestige de chez Elledue.*

Detailansicht einer Küche
Prestige von Elledue.

J-shaped kitchen
(Elledue Prestige).

*Cuisine en forme de J
Prestige de chez Elledue.*

Küche in J-Form
Prestige von Elledue.

Hinged doors on Elledue
Prestige cabinets.

*Placards avec portes abattables
Prestige de chez Elledue.*

Schrank mit heraufklappbaren
Türen Prestige von Elledue.

Slide-in range (Elledue Prestige).

*Espace cuisson avec hotte- extracteur
en maçonnerie Prestige de chez Elledue.*

Kochbereich mit Kamin für
Dunstabzug Prestige
von Elledue.

Detail of work counter in Elledue
Prestige kitchen.

*Détail du plan de travail Prestige
de chez Elledue.*

Detailansicht der Arbeitsfläche
Prestige von Elledue.

126

Alno U-shaped kitchen
with fitted cabinet with
glass doors.

*Cuisine en forme de U
avec vitrine encastrée
de chez Alno.*

Küche in U-Form mit
eingebauter Vitrine
von Alno.

Alno L shaped little
kitchen.

*Petite cuisine en forme
de L de chez Alno.*

Kleine Küche in L-Form
von Alno.

Elledue Stilnovo kitchen
with cabinets finished
in wood.

Cuisine avec finitions
en bois Stilnovo
de chez Elledue.

Küche in
Holzausfertigung
Stilnovo von Elledue.

Next page:
Alno kitchen with fitted
bodega module.

Page précédente:
Cuisine en forme de L avec
salle à manger annexée
de chez Alno.

Auf der folgenden Seite:
Küche in einer Front mit
Bodegamodul von Alno.

Elledue Stilnovo kitchen with
cabinets finished in wood.

Espace repas et alcôve
Stilnovo de chez Elledue.

Essbereich und
Speiseschrank Stilnovo
von Elledue.

Previous page:
Alno L-shaped kitchen
with dining room annex.

Page précédente:
Cuisine en forme de L avec
salle à manger annexée
de chez Alno.

Auf der vorhevigen Seite:
Küche in L-Form mit
angrenzendem Esszimmer.

Alno kitchen with central
work island.

*Cuisine avec île centrale
de Chez Alno.*

Küche mit zentraler
Insel von Alno.

Alno kitchen with
dresser annex.

*Cuisine avec alcôve
annexée de chez Alno.*

Küche mit zusätzlichem
Speiseschrank von Alno.

Alno dresser module.

Élément alcôve de chez Alno.

Speiseschrankmodul
von Alno.

Alno single island unit.

Cuisine avec un seul front de chez Alno.

Küche in einer Front von Alno.

Alno cooktop island.

Île centrale de cuisson de chez Alno.

Kochinsel von Alno.

Alno dresser module.

Cuisine en forme de L avec île centrale de travail de chez Alno.

Küche mit Kochinsel und Essbereich von Alno.

Alno L-shaped kitchen
with work island.

*Cuisine en forme de L
avec île centrale de travail
de chez Alno.*

Küche in L-Form mit
Arbeitsinsel von Alno.

Febal Risate Mod.

*Mod. Risate
de chez Febal.*

Modell Risate
von Febal.

Alno dresser module.

*Élément alcôve
de chez Alno.*

Geschiurschrankmodul
von Alno.

Febal Sinfon Mod.

Mod. Sinfon de chez Febal.

Modell Sinfon von Febal.

Febal Maya Mod.

Mod. Sinfon de chez Febal.

Modell Sinfon von Febal.

Previous page:
Detail of Febal
Sinfon Mod.

Page précédente:
Détail du mod. Sinfon
de chez Febal.

Auf der vorherigen Seite:
Detailansicht Modell
Sinfon von Febal.

Miele J-shaped kitchen.   *Cuisine en forme de J*   Küche in J-Form
                          de chez Miele.   von Miele.

Variation of the same Alno   *Variation du même modèle*   Abwandlung des gleichen
model in L-shaped form.   *en forme de L de chez Alno.*   Modells in L-Form von Alno.

Florida Paesana Mod.

Mod. Paesana de chez Florida.

Modell Paesana von Florida.

Next page:
Alno L-shaped kitchen.

*Page suivante:
Cuisine en forme de L
de chez Alno.*

Auf der folgenden Seite:
Küche in L-Form von Alno.

Febal Rosat Mod.

*Mod. Rosat
de chez Febal.*

Modell Rosat
von Febal.

Florida Paesana
Mod. cooktop.

*Espace cuisson du mod.
Paesana de chez Florida.*

Kochbereich
des Modells Paesana
von Florida.

Nobilia Cosmo Mod.

Mod. Cosmo de chez Nobilia.

Modell Cosmo von Nobilia.

Febal Casale Mod.

Mod. Casale de chez Febal.

Modell Casale von Febal.

Next page:
Miele kitchen with sink
incorporated in the
work island.

*Page suivante:
Cuisine avec île centrale
de travail et de lavage
de chez Miele.*

Auf der folgenden Seite:
Küche mit Arbeits- und
Waschinsel von Miele.

Miele kitchen in a single
cabinet series with dining
room table.

*Cuisine avec un seul front
et salle à manger adossée
de chez Miele.*

Küche in einer Front mit
angebauten Essbereich
von Miele.

Miele L-shaped kitchen
with dining room set.

*Cuisine en forme de L
avec salle à manger
de chez Miele.*

Küche in L-Form mit
Esszimmer von Miele.

Detail of work counter.

Détail d'un espace préparation.

Detailansicht des Speisenvorbereitungsbereichs.

Miele kitchen with dining room.

Ofice-cuisine de chez Miele.

Küche mit Esszimmer von Miele.

Miele kitchen with
single cabinet series.

*Cuisine avec un seul
front de chez Miele.*

Küche in einer Front
von Miele.

Leicht kitchen-dining
room.

*Office-cuisine
de chez Leicht.*

Esszimmer und küche
von Leicht.

154

Leicht L-shaped kitchen with
extractor hood.

*Cuisine en forme de L
de chez Leicht.*

Küche in L-Form mit
Dunstabzugskamin
von Leicht.

Leicht L-shaped kitchen.

Cuisine de chez Leicht.

Küche in L-Form von Leicht.

Leicht kitchen.

Cuisine de chez Leicht.

Küche von Leicht.

Leicht cooktop module.

*Élément cuisson
de chez Leicht.*

Kochmodul
von Leicht.

Leicht L-shaped kitchen.

*Cuisine en forme de L
de chez Leicht.*

Küche in L-Form
von Leicht.

Leicht L-shaped kitchen.

*Cuisine en forme de L
de chez Leicht.*

Küche in L-Form
von Leicht.

Previous page:
Siematic kitchen-dining room.

Page suivante:
Cuisine- office de chez Siematic.

Auf der vorherigen Seite:
Esszimmer und küche
von Siematic.

Leicht kitchen.

Cuisine de chez Leicht.

Küche von Leicht.

Florida Le Floglie Mod.

Mod. Le Floglie de chez Florida.

Modell Le Floglie von Florida.

Siematic central work kitchen.

Cuisine avec île centrale de chez Siematic.

Küche mit zentraler Insel von Siematic.

Florida Old Style Mod.

Mod. Old Style de chez Florida.

Modell Old Style von Florida.

Detail of Mobalpa
work island.

*Détail de l'espace travail
de chez Mobalpa.*

Detailansicht des
Arbeitsbereichs
von Mobalpa.

Nolte Antik Mod.   *Mod. Antik de chez Nolte.*   **Modell Antik von Nolte.**

Mobalpa kitchen
with fitted units.

*Cuisine avec éléments
encastrés de chez Mobalpa.*

Küche mit eingebauten
Modulen von Mobalpa.

Febal Casale Mod.

Mod. Casale de chez Febal.

Modell Casale von Febal.

Next page:
Mobalpa cooking area.

Page suivante:
Espace cuisson
de chez Mobalpa.

Auf der folgenden Seite:
Kochbereich von Mobalpa.

Nolte Country Mod.

Mod. Country de chez Nolte.

Modell Country von Nolte.

Nobilia Colorado Mod.
work area.

Espace lavage du mod.
Colorado de chez Nobilia.

Waschbereich des
Modells Colorado
von Nobilia.

Febal Bohême Mod.

Mod. Bohême de chez Febal.

Modell Bohême von Febal.

Nobilia Colorado Mod.

Mod. Colorado de chez Nobilia.

Modell Colorado von Nobilia.

Previous page:
Nolte Castell Mod.

Page précédente:
Mod. Castell de chez Nolte.

Auf der vorherigen Seite:
Modell Castell von Nolte.

Febal Conte Mod.

Mod. Conte
de chez Febal.

Modell Conte
von Febal.

Nolte Dallas 611 Mod.

Mod. Dallas 611 de chez Nolte.

Modell Dallas 611 von Nolte.

Nobilia Cortina Mod.

Mod. Cortina de chez Nobilia.

Modell Cortina von Nobilia.

170

Mobalpa Model.

Mod. de chez Mobalpa.

Modell von Mobalpa.

Mobalpa Model.

Mod. de chez Mobalpa.

Modell von Mobalpa.

Nobilia Natura Mod.

Mod. Natura de chez Nobilia.

Modell Natura von Nobilia.

Nolte Salerno Mod.

Mod. Salerno de chez Nolte.

Modell Salerno von Nolte.

Nolte Salerno Mod.

Mod. Salerno de chez Nolte.

Modell Salerno von Nolte.

Nolte Nostalgie Mod.

Mod. Nostalgia de Nolte.

Modell Nostalgie von Nolte.

Mobalpa oven
module.

*Élément four
de chez Mobalpa.*

**Herdmodul
von Mobalpa.**

Mobalpa Model.

Mod. de chez Mobalpa.

Modell von Mobalpa.

Nobilia Village Mod.

*Mod. Village
de chez Nobilia.*

**Modell Village
von Nobilia.**

Electrical Appliances / *Les appareils d'électroménager*
Elektrogeräte

The dominant is versatility. Different sizes according to today's users, fitted or freestanding, base or wall, for a single person or an entire troupe, as part of an overall design or one-off... The key is purity of line and absence of the superfluous: the uses of each element constitute luxury at its finest and the material and finish the definitive sign of style.

Leur qualité dominante est la versatilité. De différentes tailles selon les besoin de l'usager, encastrables ou indépendants, à même le sol ou surélevés, pour une seule personne ou pour un régiment, comme faisant partie d'un design globale ou comme pièce unique...On parie sur la pureté des lignes et on rejette le superflue : les prestations de chaque appareil représentent le comble du luxe et les matériaux avec lesquels ils ont été conçus le label définitif de son style.

Der dominierende Grundton ist die Flexibilität. Verschiedene Größen je nach aktuellen Benutzertyp, eingebaut oder freistehend, auf dem Boden oder in einer bestimmten Höhe, für eine Person oder ein ganzes Regiment, als Teil eines Gesamtkonzepts oder als Einzelstück.... Man setzt auf die Reinheit der Linien und verabschiedet sich vom Entbehrlichen: Die Leistungen jedes Elements ergeben die Spitze des Luxus und das Material, in welchem ausgefertigt wurde, bildet den ultimativen Stempel der Stilvorstellung.

Previous page:
Alno refrigerator with paneled door.

Page précédente:
Frigidaire avec porte
revêtue de chez Alno.

Auf der vorherigen Seite:
Kühlschrank mit Relieftür
von Alno.

Alno apartment refrigerator
with paneled door.

Frigidaire pour petit appartement
de chez Alno avec porte revêtue.

Kühlschrank für Appartments
von Alno mit Relieftür.

Cooking module and
storage with one front
by Alno.

*Élément de cuisson et
d'approvisionnement en un
seul front de chez Alno.*

Lagerungs- und
Kochmodul in einer Front
von Alno.

Mobalpa TIPI model fitted
refrigerator.

*Frigidaire encastré modèle
TIPI de chez Mobalpa.*

Eingebauter Kühlschrank
Model TIPI von Mobalpa.

Alno slide-in refrigerator.

*Frigidaire au-dessous
d'un plan de travail de
chez Alno.*

Kühlschrank unter
Arbeitsplatte von Alno.

The handles provide a
vanguardist touch in the
Whirlpool model.

*Des manettes pour un air
d'avant-garde d'un modèle
de chez Whirlpool.*

Die Griffe geben dem Modell
von Whirlpool einen
avantgardistischen Touch.

Whirlpool two-door model.

*Modèle de chez Whirlpool
avec deux portes.*

Modell von Whirlpool
mit zwei Türen.

Whirlpool dual module
freezer and refrigerator.

*Congélateur et frigidaire
en deux pièces de chez
Whirlpool.*

Gefrier-und Kühlschrank
in zwei Modulen
von Whirlpool.

Whirlpool single-door
refrigerator.

*Frigidaire avec une seule
porte de chez Whirlpool.*

Külschrank mit einer
Tür von Whirlpool.

Whirlpool two-door refrigerator
with ice-cube dispenser.

*Réfrigérateur avec deux portes
et distributeur de glaçons
Mod. de chez Whirlpool.*

Kühlschrank mit zwei Türen und
Eiswürfelspender.
Modell von Whirlpool.

Whirlpool two-door refrigerator and freezer with ice-cube dispenser.

Frigidaire et congélateur avec deux portes et distributeur de glaçons mod. de chez Whirlpool.

Kühl- und Gefriertkombination mit zwei Türen und Eisspender Modell von Whirlpool.

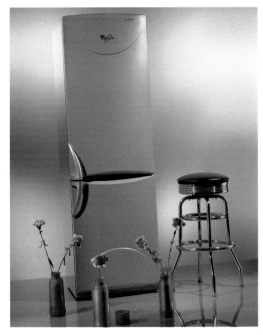

Whirlpool model in blue.

Modèle de chez Whirlpool en bleu.

Modell von Whirlpool in blau.

Rosières Ostyle 08 mod.
two-door refrigerator

*Réfrigérateur avec deux
portes mod. Ostyle 08
de chez Rosieres.*

Kühlschrank mit zwei
Türen Modell Ostyle 08
von Rosieres.

Rosières Ostyle 07 mod.
two-door refrigerator.

*Réfrigérateur avec deux
portes mod. Ostyle 07
de chez Rosieres.*

Kühlschrank mit zwei
Türen Modell Ostyle 07
von Rosieres.

Rosières Ostyle 09 mod.
two-door refrigerator.

*Réfrigérateur avec deux
portes mod. Ostyle 09
de chez Rosieres.*

Kühlschrank mit zwei
Türen Modell Ostyle 09
von Rosieres.

Rosières Ostyle 10 mod.
two-door refrigerator.

Frigidaire avec deux portes mod.
Ostyle 10 de chez Rosieres.

Kühlschrank mit zwei Türen
Modell Ostyle 10 von Rosieres.

The color of these
Whirlpool models changes
with the light.

La couleur de ces modèles
de Whirlpool chargent
avec la lumière.

Die Farbe dieser Modelle
von Whirlpool wechselt
je nach Licht.

An easygoing presentation
for a high-tech model.

Une présentation amusante
pour un modèle de haute
technologie.

Eine ungezwungene
Presentation für ein
hochtechnisches Modell.

The Whirlpool mod. here
includes a clock in the top door.

*Ce modèle de chez Whirlpool
a une horloge incorporée dans
la partie supérieure.*

Das Modell von Whirlpool fügt
eine Uhr in die obere Tür ein.

The Daewoo Mod.
FR-700CB with retro
color and design.

*Mod. FR-700CB de chez
Daewoo avec un air rétro
autant dans la forme
comme dans la couleur.*

Modell FR-700CB von
Daewo mit altem
Aussehen in Farbe und
Design.

The Zanussi OZ mod. breaks
with the regularity of
conventional forms.

*Le mod. OZ de chez Zanussi
romps avec la régularité des
formes conventionnelles.*

Das Modell OZ von Zanussi
bricht mit der
RegelmäBigkeit der
konventionellen Formen.

The Gaggenau bodega
refrigerator is for restaurants
and sybarites.

*Le réfrigérateur cellier de chez
Gaggenau a été conçu pour
les restaurants et les grands
gourmets.*

Der Bodegakühlschrank von
Gaggenau, gedacht für
Restaurants und GenieBer.

Alno decorative extractor in a corner.

Hotte décorative de chez Alno encastrée dans un coin.

Dekorativer Dunstabzug von Alno, eingepaßt in eine Ecke.

Alno extractor hood in stainless steel with grill shelving.

Hotte-extracteur de chez Alno en acier inoxydable avec étagères auxiliaires en grillage.

Dunstabzugshaube von Alno aus rostfreiem Stahl mit Hilfsgitterregalen.

Siemens hood with three halogen lamps.

Hotte de chez Siemens avec trois oeils de boeuf halogènes.

Dunstabzugshaube von Siemens mit drei Halogenleuchten.

Original hip-roof hood
with visor by Alno.

*Hotte très originale avec
visière sur le devant
de chez Alno.*

Originaller Dunstabzug
im Stile eines Daches
von Alno.

Alno decorative hood
in stainless steel.

*Hotte décorative de chez
Alno en acier inoxydable.*

Dekorative
Dunstabzugshaube von
Alno aus rostfreien Stahl.

This Alno hood keeps its
extracting power on the
lower surface.

*Cette hotte de chez Alno
maintient la puissance de
l'extracteur sur une
superficie inférieure.*

Dieser Dunstabzug von
Alno behält seine
Leistung trotz kleinerer
Oberfläche.

Siemens LC 75955 Mod.
decorative extractor hood.

Hotte décorative mod.
LC 75955 de chez Siemens.

Dekorative Dunstabzug
Modell LC 75955 von Siemens.

Siemens LC 56950 Mod.
decorative extractor hood.

Hotte décorative mod.
LC 56950 de chez Siemens.

Dekorative Dunstabzug
Modell LC 56950 von Siemens.

Siemens LC 85950 Mod.
decorative extractor hood.

Hotte décorative mod.
LC. 85950 de chez Siemens.

Dekorative Dunstabzug
Modell LC 85950 von Siemens.

Siemens LC 56650 Mod.
decorative extractor hood.

Hotte décorative mod.
LC. 56650 de chez Siemens.

Dekorative Dunstabzugs
Modell LC 56650 von Siemens.

Alno decorative
extractor hood.

*Hotte décorative
de chez Alno.*

Dekorative Dunstabzug
von Alno.

Siemens LC 80950 Mod.
steel and glass decorative
hood.

*Hotte décorative en acier et
verre mod. LC. 80950 de
chez Siemens.*

Dekorativer Dunstabzug
aus Stahl und Glas Modell
LC 80950 von Siemens.

Siemens SM835 Mod.
decorative steel extractor
hood.

*Hotte décorative en acier
mod. SM 835 de chez
Siemens.*

Dekorativer Dunstabzug
aus Stahl Modell SM835
von Siemens.

Siemens SM796 Mod. ultrathin design for a high-potency hood.

Design ultraplat pour une hotte de grande puissance. Mod. SM796 de chez Siemens.

Extraflaches Design für eine Dunstabzugshaube mit starker Leistung. Modell SM796 von Siemens.

Alno ultradynamic design hood mod. for big kitchens.

Hotte de design ultradipanique pour grande cuisine de chez Alno.

Dunstabzug mit dynamischen Design für groBe Küchen. Modell von Alno.

Whirlpool integrated model hood.

Hotte intégrée mod. de chez Whirlpool.

Integrierte Dunstabzug Modell von Whirlpool.

Nolte decorative extractor for kitchen islands.

Hotte décorative pour île central de cuisson mod. de chez Nolte.

Dekorative Dunstabzug für Kochinseln Modell von Nolte.

The power of steel is lighter
in Alno's minimalist design.

*La force de l'acier devient
plus légère avec une création
minimaliste.*

**Die Kraft des Stahls wird
durch minimalistisches
Design abgemildert
von Alno.**

Leicht hanging hood
with shelves.

*Hotte suspendue au
plafond avec des étagères
de chez Leicht.*

Von der Decke hängende
Dunstabzugshaube
mit angebauten
Regalen von Leicht.

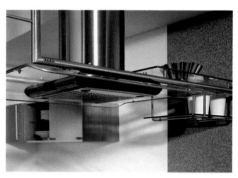

The glass hood over the cooking
area is a lightweight Alno model.

*La hotte en verre sur la superficie
d'extraction rend léger ce modèle
de chez Alno.*

Der Dunstabzug aus Glas über der
Abzugsoberfläche verleiht
dem Modell von Alno Leichtigkeit.

Slide-in cooktop and oven
in the same Alno module.

*Plaque de cuisson et four
encastré dans le même
élément de chez Alno.*

Kochfeld und eingebauter
Ofen im gleichen Modul,
von Alno.

Matching cooktop and oven
with drawered cabinet
by Alno.

*Four et plaque de cuisson
coordonnés avec les tiroirs
et les tireurs de chez Alno.*

Ofen und Kochfeld mit
dazu passender
Schubladen- und
Fächerfront von Alno.

Siemens Model
HB 89E44 oven.

*Four mod. HB 89 E44
de chez Siemens.*

Ofen Modell
HB 89E44 von Siemens.

Siemens Model HB
66E44 oven.

*Four mod. HB 66 E44 de
chez Siemens.*

Ofen Modell HB 66E44
von Siemens.

Leicht module
with microwave
and oven.

*Élément micro-on-
des et four de chez
Leicht.*

Modul mit
Mikrowelle und
Ofen von Leicht.

Siemens Model
HB 66E24 oven.

*Four mod. HB 66 E24
de chez Siemens.*

Ofen Modell HB 66E24
von Siemens.

Siemens Model
HB 66E54 oven.

Four mod. HB 66 E54
de chez Siemens.

Modell HB 66E54
von Siemens.

Siemens Model
HB 66E64 oven.

Four mod. HB 66 E64
de chez Siemens.

Ofen Modell HB 66E64
von Siemens.

Siemens Model
HB 79E24 oven.

Mod. HB 79 E24
de chez Siemens.

Modell HB 79E24
von Siemens.

Whirlpool multi-use oven
Model AKP 500.

*Four multifonctions mod.
AKP 500 de chez Whirlpool.*

Multifunktionaler Ofen
Modell AKP 500 von
Whirlpool.

Whirlpool multi-use oven
Model AKP 525.

*Four multifonctions mod.
AKP 525 de chez Whirlpool.*

Multifunktionaler Ofen
Modell AKP 525 von
Whirlpool.

Whirlpool multi-use oven Model
AKP 634.

*Four multifonctions mod. AKP 634
de chez Whirlpool.*

Multifunktionaler Ofen
Modell AKP 634 von Whirlpool.

Whirlpool multi-use oven
Model AKP 636.

*Four multifonctions mod. AKP 636
de chez Whirlpool.*

Multifunktionaler Ofen Modell
AKP 636 von Whirlpool.

Whirlpool fitted oven,
Model AKZ 144.

*Four encastrable mod. AKZ 144
de chez Whirlpool.*

Einbaubarer Ofen
Modell AKZ 144 von Whirlpool.

Whirlpool wide oven,
Model AKG 637.

*Four extra-large mod. AKG 637
de chez Whirlpool.*

Extra breiter Ofen
Modell AKG 637 von Whirlpool.

Whirlpool oven,
Model AKP 638.

*Four mod. AKP 638
de chez Whirlpool.*

Ofen Modell AKP 638
von Whirlpool.

Whirlpool counter oven,
Model COM.

*Four-plaque de cuisson mod.
COM de chez Whirlpool.*

Ofen mit Arbeitsplatte
Modell COM von Whirlpool.

Siemens multi-use
oven.

*Four multifonctions
de chez Siemens.*

Multifunktionaler Ofen
von Siemens.

Nolte microwave
oven.

*Four micro-ondes
de chez Nolte.*

Mikrowellenofen
von Nolte.

Alno high fitted oven.

*Four encastré en hauteur
de chez Alno.*

FHoch eingebauter Ofen
von Alno.

Whirlpool AKZ 144 fitted
electric oven.

*Four électrique encastré
mod. AKZ 144 de chez
Whirlpool.*

Eingebauter elektrischer
Ofen Modell AKZ 144
von Whirlpool.

Siemens HB 79E64 oven.

Four mod. HB 79 E64 de chez Siemens.

Ofen Modell HB 79E64 von Siemens.

Siemens HE 37064 oven.

Four mod. HE 37064 de chez Siemens.

Ofen Modell HE 37064 von Siemens.

Siemens HE 56054 oven.

Four mod. HE 56054 de chez Siemens.

Ofen Modell HE 56054 von Siemens..

Siemens HE 56E64 oven.

Four mod. HE 56 E64 de chez Siemens.

Ofen Modell HE 56E64 von Siemens.

Siemens HE 56024 oven.

Four mod. HE 56024 de chez Siemens.

Ofen Modell HE 56024 von Siemens.

Siemens HE 56044 oven.

Four mod. HE 56044 de chez Siemens.

Ofen Modell HE 56044 von Siemens.

Siemens HE 68E44 oven.

Four mod. HE 68 E44 de chez Siemens.

Ofen Modell HE 68E44 von Siemens.

Siemens HE 89E54 oven.

Four mod. HE 89E54 de chez Siemens.

Ofen Modell HE *89E54* von Siemens.

Alno ZANKER model
fitted oven.

*Four encastré mod.
Zanker de chez Alno.*

Eingebauter Ofen
Modell ZANKER
von Alno.

Whirlpool oven and
microwave with steel
doors.

*Four et micro-ondes avec
portes d'acier mod.
de chez Whirlpool.*

Ofen und Mikrowelle mit
Stahltüren Modell
von Whirlpool.

Alno fitted storage
model with oven.

*Élément rangement
avec four encastré mod.
de chez Alno.*

Aufbewahrungsmodul mit
eingebautem Ofen,
Modell von Alno.

212

Siemens SM863
two-door oven.

*Four de deux portes
mod. SM 863 de chez Siemens.*

Zweitüriger Ofen
Modell SM863 von Siemens.

Alno independent
fitted counter oven.

*Four indépendant
encastré en hauteur
de chez Alno.*

Unabhängiger, hoch
eingebauter Ofen
von Alno.

Siemens SM070 stainless
steel electric oven.

*Four électrique en acier
inoxydable mod. SM 070
de chez Siemens.*

Elektrischer Ofen aus
rostfreien Stahl Modell
SM070 von Siemens.

Mobalpa Sarila model:
counter height fitted
oven and microwave.

*Four et micro-ondes
encastrés en hauteur
mod. Sarila
de chez Mobalpa.*

Hoch eingebauter Ofen
und Mikrowelle
Modell Sarila
von Mobalpa.

Siemens module with
cooktop, oven and hood.

*Plan de cuisson avec
plaque, four et hotte
de chez Siemens.*

Kochfront mit Kochfeld,
Ofen und Dunstabzug
von Siemens.

Siemens SM887 fitted oven
with hinged door.

*Four encastré avec porte
abattable mod. SM 887
de chez Siemens.*

Eingebauter Ofen mit
herunterklappbarer Tür
Modell SM887
von Siemens.

Alno slide-in
dishwasher with
panel door.

*Lave-vaisselle intégré
au-dessous d'un évier
avec porte revêtue
de chez Alno.*

Intergrierter
Geschirrspüler unter
Arbeitsplatte mit
Relieftür von Alno.

Alno slide-in dishwasher
with panel door.

*Lave-vaisselle au-dessous
d'un évier avec porte
revêtue de chez Alno.*

Geschirrspüler unter
Spüle mit Relieftür
von Alno.

Alno slide-in dishwasher
with panel door.

*Lave-vaisselle intégré
avec porte revêtue de
chez Alno.*

Intergrierter
Geschirrspüler mit
Relieftür von Alno.

Alno family counter
height dishwasher
with drawers.

*Lave-vaisselle familial
élevé dans un élément
avec tiroirs de chez Alno.*

Angehobener
Familiengeschirrspüler in
Modul mit Schubladen
von Alno.

Mobalpa fitted
mini-dishwasher.

*Lave-vaisselle encastré
pour petites quantités
de chez Mobalpa.*

Eingebauter
Geschirrspüler für
wenige Benutzer
von Mobalpa.

Alno fitted and paneled
mini-dishwasher.

*Mini lave-vaisselle
encastré et revêtu
de chez Alno.*

Engebauter,
Minigeschirrspüler
von Alno.

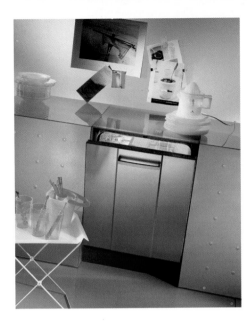

Whirlpool lean-open
dishwasher.

*Original orifice
d'ouverture chez
Whirlpool.*

Orginelle Öffnung im
Geschirrspüler
von Whirlpool.

Whirlpool slide-in dishwasher.

*Lave-vaisselle intégré dans un
front de cuisine de chez
Whirlpool.*

In die Küchenfront intergrierter
Geschirrspüler von Whirlpool.

Whirlpool dishwasher.

*Lave-vaisselle de chez
Whirlppol.*

Spülmaschine
von Whirlpool.

Whirlpool dishwasher.

*Lave-vaisselle de chez
Whirlppol.*

Spülmaschine
von Whirlpool.

Alno fitted counter level
dishwasher.

*Lave-vaisselle intégré
au-dessous d'un évier
de chez Alno.*

Unter der Spüle
intergrierter
Geschirrspüler von Alno.

Alno slide-in base level
dishwasher.

*Lave-vaisselle sous plan
de travail de chez Alno.*

Geschirrspüler unter
Arbeitsplatte von Alno.

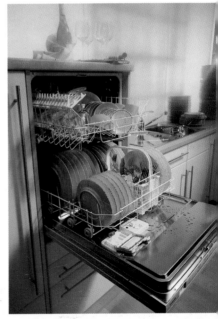

Alno fitted counter level
dishwasher.

*Lave-vaisselle
au-dessous d'une plaque
de cuisson de chez Alno.*

In ein Hochmodul
eingebauter
Geschirrspüler von Alno.

Alno family dishwasher.

*Lave-vaisselle familial
de chez Alno.*

Familiengeschirrspüler
von Alno.

Whirlpool dishwasher
with concealed controls.

*Lave-vaisselle avec
commandes cachés
de chez Whirlpool.*

Geschirrspüler mit
unauffälligen
Bedienungsschaltern,
Modell von whirlpool.

Alno sink with integrated
small dishwasher
and drainer.

*Évier avec égouttoir et petit
lave-vaisselle intégré
de chez Alno.*

Spüle mit Abtropffläche
und kleinem integrierten
Geschirrspüler von Alno.

Whirlpool's latest model
refrigerators, dishwashers,
and cooktops.

*Derniers modèles de
réfrigérateurs,
lave-vaisselles et plaques
de cuisson de chez Whirlpool.*

Der letzten Modelle für
Kühlung, Spüle und Kochen
von Whirlpool.

Whirlpool large-capacity
washing machine.

*Machine à laver de
grande capacité
de chez Whirlpool.*

Waschmaschine mit
groβer Kapazität
von Whirlpool.

Whirlpool column
dishwasher and drier.

*Machine à laver et
sèche-linge en colonne
de chez Whirlpool.*

Geschirrspüler und
Trockner als Säule
von Whirlpool.

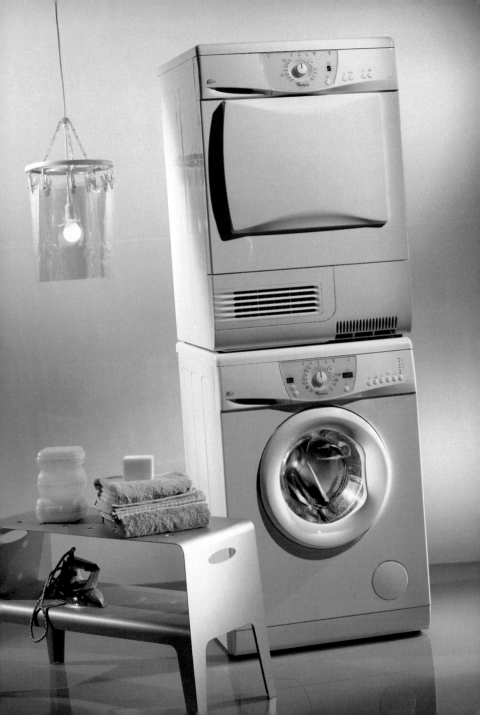

Whirlpool front-loading
washing machine.

*Machine à laver de charge
frontale mod. de chez Whirlppol.*

Waschmaschine mit
Frontbeladung
Modell von Whirlpool.

Whirlpool drier.

Sèche-linge de chez Whirlpool.

Trockner Modell von Whirlpool.

Whirlpool top-loading
washing machine.

*Machine à laver
de charge supérieure
de chez Whirlpool.*

Oberladerwaschmaschine
Modell von Whirlpool.

Siemens HF 87960
microwave oven.

*Four micro-ondes mod. HF 87960
de chez Siemens.*

Mikrowellenherd
Modell HF 87960 von Siemens.

Siemens HF 66061
microwave oven.

*Four micro-ondes mod.
HF 66061 de chez Siemens.*

Mikrowellenherd
Modell HF 66061 von Siemens.

Siemens HF 87950
microwave oven.

*Four micro-ondes mod.
HF 87950 de chez Siemens.*

Mikrowellenherd
Modell HF 87950 von Siemens.

Siemens HF 87940
microwave oven.

*Four micro-ondes mod.
HF 87940 de chez Siemens.*

Mikrowellenherd
Modell HF 87940 von Siemens.

Whirlpool MAXIMO
model microwave oven.

*Four micro-ondes mod.
Maximo de chez
Whirlpool.*

Mikrowellenherd Modell
MAXIMO von Whirlpool.

Siemens HF 66051 microwave oven.

Four micro-ondes mod. HF 66051 de chez Siemens.

Mikrowellenherd
Modell HF 66051 von Siemens.

Siemens HF 66041
microwave oven.

*Four micro-ondes mod.
HF 66041 de chez Siemens.*

Mikrowellenherd
Modell HF 66041
von Siemens.

Siemens HF 26561
microwave oven.

*Four micro-ondes mod.
HF 26561 de chez Siemens.*

Mikrowellenherd
Modell HF 26561
von Siemens.

Siemens HF 23520 microwave oven.

Four micro-ondes mod. HF 23520 de chez Siemens.

Mikrowellenherd
Modell HF 23520 von Siemens.

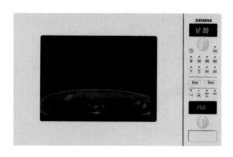

Siemens HF 66021
microwave oven.

Four micro-ondes mod.
66021 de chez Siemens.

Mikrowellenherd
Modell HF 66021 von
Siemens.

Siemens HF 23550microwave oven.

Four micro-ondes mod. 23550
de chez Siemens.

Mikrowellenherd
Modell HF 23550 von Siemens.

Siemens HF 26551
microwave oven.

Four micro-ondes mod.
26551 de chez Siemens.

Mikrowellenherd
Modell HF 26551 von
Siemens.

Solutions for order / *Des solutions pour le rangement.* Lösungen für die Ordnung

"A place for everything and everything in its place" is the rule of thumb in the design of container furniture. Closets, drawers and pantries are a display of ingenuity to resolve the rational distribution of utensils, receptacles and food according to weight, size and frequency of use. The inside of each unit is subjected to a rigorous analysis so that no surface is excluded from the mission of ordering and distribution. Auxiliary elements for small objects (hangers, hooks or bars) enhance their function with a touch of style in their design.

" Chaque chose à sa place ". C'est la maxime actuelle à suivre dans la création des meubles de rangement. Placards, tiroirs et alcôves possèdent un haut degré d'imagination destiné à solutionner les problèmes de distribution rationnelle des ustensiles de cuisine, récipients et aliments selon leur poids, taille et fréquence d'utilisation. L'intérieur de chaque élément est soumis à une analyse rigoureuse dans le but d'utiliser sans omission chaque coin de la superficie dans leur fonction d'ordre et de distribution. Les éléments auxiliaires pour petits objets (crochets à vêtements et barres) conjuguent leur fonction avec une touche de style dans leur design.

"Ein Platz für jedes Ding und ein jedes Ding an seinen Platz ", das ist der rechtskräftige Leitsatz für Möbel zur Aufbewahrung. Vitrinen, Schubladen, Speiseschränke sind der Aufmarsch der Erfindungsgabe um die rationale Verteilung von Utensilien, Behälter und Lebensmittel je nach GröBe, Gewicht und Gebrauchshäufigkeit zu gewährleisten. Das Innere jedes Moduls wird einer rigurosen Analyse unterworfen um sicherzustellen, daB kein Raum bei der Ordnungs- und Verteilmission übrigbleibt. Zusätzliche Elemente für kleineve objekte (kaken, henkel oder Leisten) werten ihre Funktion durch einen Touch ihres stils auf.

Previous page:
Nolte Star kitchen.

Page précédente:
Cuisine Star
de chez Nolte.

Auf der vorherigen Seite:
Küche Star von Nolte.

Metallic rod with hooks
for utensils by Nolte.

Barre métallique avec crochets
pour ustensiles de chez Nolte.

Metalleiste mit Haken
für Utensilien von Nolte.

Closets   *Les placards*   Schränke

Kitchen cabinets, designed according to a modular scheme, maintain successful features with new combinations to take advantage of corners, using pull-out structures made of ultra-lightweight materials, as well as independent pieces which break up the continuous front (circular work units with wooden surface), seeking pragmatism in folding or collapsible doors and in the addition of elements more in keeping with other rooms (filing cabinets, structured glass display cases, decorative shelves, ...).

Les placards de cuisines, créer selon un schémas modulaire, proposent avec succès de nouvelles combinaisons qui profitent de tous les coins moyennant des structures escamotables faites de matériaux ultralégers, ainsi que de pièces indépendantes qui rompent avec les plans de travail continus (éléments de travail circulaires avec plan de travail en bois), recherchant le pragmatisme dans les portes pliantes ou abattables tout en ajoutant des éléments plus caractéristiques d'autres pièces de la maison. (meubles classeurs, vitrines en verre structuré, étagères décoratives...).

Küchenschränke, entworfen nach dem Modulschema, bieten erfolgreiche Vorschläge durch neue Kombinationen, welche auch den letzten Winkel mittels ausziehbaren Strukturen und ultraleichten Materialien ausnützen oder welche durch unabhängige Teile die Kontinuität der Front brechen (kreisförmige Arbeitsmodule mit Holzauflage), während sie den Pragmatismus in zusammen- oder herunterklappbaren Türen genauso wie in der Addition von aus anderen Teilen der Wohnung herangeführten Elementen (Aktenschränke, strukturierte Glasvitrinen, dekorative Regale,...) suchen .

Previous page:
Closet with guillotine door
by Tielsa.

Page précédente:
Placard avec porte guillotine
de chez Tielsa.

Auf der vorherigen Seite:
Schrank mit nach oben zu
öffnender Schiebetür von Tielsa.

3 door display
cabinet by Alno.

Placard vitrine à trois
portes de chez Alno.

Vitrinenschrank mit drei
Türen von Alno.

Tielsa cabinets with independent
glass shelves.

*Placard de chez Tielsa avec des
étagères en verre indépendantes*

Schränke von Tielsa mit
unabhängigen Glasregalen.

Unit with sliding
door by Alno.

Elément avec porte
coulissante de chez Alno.

Modul mit Schiebetür
von Alno.

Display cabinet with
interior light by Tielsa.

Vitrine avec éclairage
intérieure de chez Tielsa.

Vitrine mit
Innenbeleuchtung
von Tielsa.

Corner base cabinet with
semi-circular shelves
by Alno.

*Placard en coin avec
étagères demi-circulaires
de chez Alno.*

Eckschrank mit
halbrunden Regalbrettern
von Alno.

Closet with spice rack on
the inside by Alno.

*Placard pour épices dans
la partie intérieure
de chez Alno.*

*Schrank mit internen
Gewürzständer von Alno.*

Unit with
panel door
by Alno.

*Élément
escamotable avec
porte revêtue
de chez Alno.*

Ausziehbares
Modul mit
Relieftür von
Alno.

Upper unit with folding
semi-opaque door by Alno.

*Élément supérieur avec porte demi
opaque et pliante de chez Alno.*

Hochmodul mit halbmatter
klappbarer Tür von Alno.

Double shelf inside
lower unit by Mobalpa.

*Double étagère dans la partie
intérieure d'un élément bas
de chez Mobalpa.*

Doppeltes Regalbrett im
Inneren des Niedermoduls
von Mobalpa.

Corner unit with revolving
shelves and dividers by Leicht.

*Meuble d'angle avec des
étagères tournantes et
séparations de chez Leicht.*

Eckschrank mit drehbahren
Regalbrettern und Separatoren
von Leicht.

Single door display cabinet
Tipi model by Mobalpa.

*Vitrine d'une seule porte
mod. Tipi de chez Mopalpa.*

Eintürige Vitrine Model Tipi
von Mobalpa.

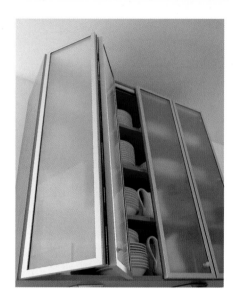

Circular work
surface with revolving
interior by Alno.

*Pan de travail circulaire
avec intérieur tournant
de chez Alno.*

Runde Aubeitsplatte
mit drehbaven Regalen
von Alno.

Unit with double folding
door by Alno.

Élément avec double
porte pliante
de chez Alno.

Modul mit klappbarer
Doppeltür von Alno.

Detail of folding
door by Alno.

*Détail d'une porte
abattable de chez Alno.*

Detailansicht einer
herunterklappbaren
Tür von Alno.

Series of shelves
between units by Alno.

*Série d'étagères entre
éléments de chez Alno.*

Regalserie zwischen
Modulen von Alno.

246

Unit with 4 shelves and
drawers by Alno.

*Élément de 4 étagères et
tiroirs de chez Alno.*

Modul mit 4 Regalen und
Schubladen von Alno.

Unit with 4 filing shelves
by Alno.

*Élément de 4 tiroirs et
meubles classeurs
de chez Alno.*

Modul mit 4
Aktenschubladen
von Alno.

Display cabinet with
metallic legs by Leicht.

*Placard vitrine avec pattes
métalliques de chez Leicht.*

Vitrinenschrank mit
MetallfüBen von Leicht.

Series of units and
shelves by Leicht.

*Série d'éléments et
étagères de chez Leicht.*

Serie von Modulen und
Regalen von Leicht.

Series of shelves between
units by Alno.

*Série d'éléments carrés
de chez Alno.*

Serie von quadratischen
Modulen von Alno.

Two door display
cabinet by Alno.

*Vitrine de 2 portes
de chez Alno.*

**Zweitürige Vitrine
von Alno.**

Pantry closet with double
folding door by Febal.

*Placard garde-manger
avec double porte pliante
de chez Febal.*

Speiseschrank mit
doppelter klappbarer
Tür von Febal.

Detail of modular
shelf unit by Alno.

Détail d'étagère
modulaire de chez Alno.

Detailansicht eines
Modulregals von Alno.

Next page
Baldachin with double
shelf and metallic support by
Leicht-Alsa.

Page suivante:
Baldaquin avec double
étagère et support métallique
de chez Leicht-Alsa

Auf der folgenden Seite:
Baldachin mit doppeltem
Regalbrett und Metallstütze
von Leicht-Alsa.

Cabinet with folding
door in white by Alno.

*Placard avec porte pliarte
en blanc de chez Alno.*

Weißer Schrank mit
klappbarer Tür von Alno.

Cabinet with folding
doors and light above
counter top by Alno.

*Placard avec portes
pliables et éclairage
sur le plan de travail
de chez Alno.*

Schrank mit klappbaren
Türen und Licht über
Arbeitsplatte von Alno.

Corner unit with work board
and circular shelves by Alno.

*Placard en coin avec table
de travail et étagères
circulaires de chez Alno.*

Eckmodul mit Arbeitsplatte
und kreisförmigen
Regalbrettern von Alno.

Cabinet with double pull-out
cart by Mobalpa.

*Placard avec double chariot
escamotable de chez Mobalpa.*

Schrank mit doppeltem, ausziehbarem
Fahrgestell von Mobalpa.

Circular unit for
receptacles by Alno.

*Élément circulaire pour
récipient de chez Alno.*

Kreisförmiges Modul
für Behälter von Alno.

Set of units of
different heights by Alno.

*Ensemble d'éléments de
différentes hauteurs de chez Alno.*

Ensemble von verschiedenen
Modulen verschiedener Höhe von Alno.

| Units with folding door by Mobalpa. | *Élément avec porte pliante de chez Mobalpa.* | Module mit klappbarer Tür von Mobalpa. | Unit for draining board with folding door by Alno. | *Élément avec égouttoir et porte abattable de chez Alno.* | Modul für Abtropfsieb mit herunterklappbarer Tür von Alno. |

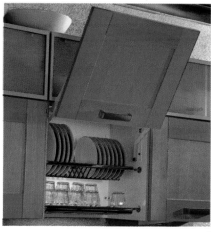

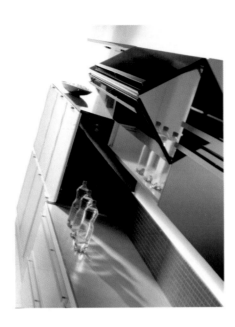

Sarila model by Mobalpa.

*Modèle Sarila
de chez Mobalpa.*

Modell Sarila
von Mobalpa.

Low display case
units by Mobalpa.

*Élément vitrine bas
de chez Mobalpa.*

Vitrinenniedermodule
von Mobalpa.

Metallic shelves
by Mobalpa.

*Étagères métalliques
de chez Mobalpa.*

Mettalregale
von Mobalpa.

Upper units with folding
doors by Mobalpa.

*Éléments supérieurs avec
portes pliantes
de chez Mobalpa.*

Hochmodule mit klappbaren
Türen von Mobalpa.

Over counter top unit
by Mobalpa.

*Élément sur plaque de
cuisson de chez Mobalpa.*

Modul überArbeitsplatte
von Mobalpa.

Unit with laminated
wood shelves by Nolte.

*Élément avec étagères
en bois plaqué de chez Nolte.*

Modul mit laminierten
Holzregalbrettern von Nolte.

258

Corner work unit
by Nolte.

*Coin de travail
de chez Nolte.*

Arbeitsecktisch
von Nolte.

Unit with shutter closure
by Alno.

*Élément avec fermeture
volet de chez Alno.*

Modul mit
Jalousieschutz von Alno.

Detail of display case by Mobalpa.

*Détail d'une vitrine
de chez Mopbalpa.*

Detailansicht einer Vitrine
von Mobalpa.

4 door unit
by Mobalpa.

*Élément de 4 portes
de chez Mobalpa.*

Modul mit 4 Türen
von Mobalpa.

Unit with 4 shelves
by Alno.

*Élément de 4 étagères
de chez Alno.*

Modul mit 4 Regalen
von Alno.

Pull-out corner
unit by Alno.

*Élément de coin
escamotable de chez Alno.*

Ausziehbares Eckmodul
von Alno.

Side cabinet for work
island by Leicht.

*Placards latéraux pour
île centrale de travail
de chez Leicht.*

Seitenschränke für
Arbeitsinsel von Leicht.

Sideboard unit
Sarila model by Mobalpa.

*Élément buffet mod.
Sarila de chez Mobalpa.*

Sidebordmodul
Modell Sarila
von Mobalpa.

Display case with sliding
door by Mobalpa.

*Vitrine avec porte
coulissante
de chez Mobalpa.*

Vitrine mit
Schiebetür
von Mobalpa.

Display case unit with 4
shelves by Mobalpa.

*Élément vitrine avec 4
étagères de chez
Mobalpa.*

Vitrinenmodul mit 4
Regalbrettern
von Mobalpa.

Drawers   Les tiroirs   Schubladen

The space below the counter top is organized in drawers with different heights, from the flat drawer for knives to the extra-deep drawers for plates and pans, with convenient dividers and buffers to avoid slippages when opening. Different levels also fit inside in the form of pull-out trays. The drawers become organizers thanks to the multiple insertable models for cutlery, spice racks and other kitchen utensils,... even small electrical appliances with socket inside. Lastly, refrigerated drawers are the latest thing in modern kitchens.

L'espace existant au-dessous du plan de travail se divise en tiroirs de différentes hauteurs, depuis le plus plat pour les couteaux au compartiments les plus profonds pour assiettes et casseroles avec les séparations nécessaires et des stop qui évitent le glissement des tiroirs en les ouvrant. On peut aussi y trouver à l'intérieur différents nivaux sous forme de plateaux escamotables. Les tiroirs deviennent les principaux organisateurs de l'espace grâce aux multiples accessoires pour les couverts, compartiments à épices et tout d'autres ustensiles de cuisine,...et même pour des petit appareils d'électroménagers avec une prise de courant à l'intérieur. Finalement, les tiroirs réfrigérateurs son le non plus ultra des cuisines modernes.

Den Raum unterhalb der Arbeitsfläche gestalten Schubladen in verschiedenen GröBen, angefangen von ganz flachen für Messer bis hin zu extratiefen Schubfächern für Teller und Kochtöpfe, mit zweckmäBigen Seperatoren und Puffern, welche das Abrutschen der Schubladen beim Öffnen verhindern. Durch herausnehmbare Schubfächer passen in das Innere auch verschiedene Ebenen. Die Schubladen werden zu Organisatoren, dank der multiplen, einsetzbaren Modelle für Besteck, Gewürzständer sowie sonstige der Küche eigene Nützlichkeiten.... bis hin zu kleinen Elektrogeräten mit eigenem Stromabnehmer im Schubladeninneren. Der letzte Schrei der modernen Küche sind gekühlte Schubladenfächer.

Previous page:
Organizer for cutlery and
vegetables by Mobalpa.

Page précédente:
Organisateur pour couverts
et féculents.

Auf der vorherigen Seite:
Organisator für Besteck und
Gemüse von Mobalpa.

Drawers with dividers by Nolte.

Tiroirs avec séparations
de chez Nolte.

Schubladen mit Seperatoren
von Nolte.

Recycling unit with 3
bins by Alno.

*Élément avec 3 poubelles
de recyclage de chez Alno.*

Recyclingmodul mit drei
Behältern von Alno.

Unit with 3 recycling bins
by Alno.

*Élément avec 3 poubelles
de recyclage de chez Alno.*

Recyclingmodul mit drei
Behältern von Alno

Pull-out unit with bin
and shelf by Alno.

*Élément escamotable avec
poubelle et étagère de chez Alno.*

Herausziehbaves Modul mit
Eimer und Regal von Alno.

Drawer for cutlery and spice rack by Alno.

Tiroir pour couverts et épices de chez Alno.

Schublade für Besteck und Gewürze von Alno.

Flat drawer for trays by Alno.

Tiroir plat pour plateaux de chez Alno.

Schublade für Besteck von Alno.

Next page:
Filing cabinet type
drawer by Alno.

Drawer for large
receptacles by Alno.

*Page suivante:
Tiroirs type meubles
classeurs de chez Alno.*

Drawer for cutlery by Alno.

Tiroir pour couverts de chez Alno.

Flache Schublade für Tabletts von Alno.

*Compartiments pour grands
récipients de chez Alno.*

**Auf der folgenden Seite:
Schublade im Stile eines
Aktenschranks
von Alno.**

**Schubfach für groBe Behälter
von Alno.**

Pull-out refrigerated
drawer by Tielsa.

*Tiroir frigidaire escamotable
de chez Tielsa.*

Herausziehbare
Kühlschrankschublade
von Tielsa.

Receptacles with lid by Alno.

Récipients avec couvercle de chez Alno.

Behälter mit Deckel von Alno.

Next page:
Intermediate drawer with
anti-slip dividers.

Page suivante:
Tiroir intermédiaire avec
séparations antiglissantes.

Auf der folgenden Seite:
Mittlere Schublade mit
rutschfesten Seperatoren.

Drawer with unit for
jars by Leicht.

*Tiroir avec élément pour
pots de chez Liecht.*

Schublade mit Modul für
Einmachgläser von Leicht.

Double width drawer for
cutlery and spices.

*Double tiroir pour couverts
et épices.*

Doppelte breite Schublade
für Besteck und Gewürze.

Unit with 3 plasticized
shelves by Alno.

*Élément avec 3 tiroirs
plastifiés de chez Alno.*

Modul mit drei plastifizierten
Schubladen von Alno.

Drawers for pans
by Alno.

*Compartiments pour
casseroles de chez Alno.*

Schubfächer für
Kochtöpfe von Alno.

Below counter top drawers
by Mobalpa.

*Compartiments au-dessous
d'un plan de travail de chez
Mobalpa.*

Schubfächer unter
Arbeitsplatte von Mobalpa.

Double width drawer
with dividers by Poggen.

*Compartiment extra large
avec séparations
de chez Poggen.*

Doppeltes, breites
Schubfach mit
Separatoren von Poggen.

Drawer for tea towels and
dishcloths by Alno.

Tiroir pour torchons de chez Alno.

Schublade für Tücher von Alno.

Drawer with
curved front by
Leicht.

*Compartiment
courbé de chez
Leicht.*

Schubfach mit
gerundeter Front
von Leicht.

Drawer with panel
front by Alno.

*Compartiment avec front
revêtu de chez Alno.*

Schubfach mit
Relieffuont von Alno.

Drawer with dividing
pivots by Leicht.

*Tiroir avec séparations
pivotantes de chez Leicht.*

Schublade mit
Separatorzapfen
von Leicht.

Drawer with support for
cutter by Leicht.

*Tiroir avec support
pour machine à couper
de chez Alno.*

Schublade mit Träger
für Schneidegerät
von Alno.

Drawer with curved
front by Leicht.

*Compartiment avec front
courbée de chez Leicht.*

Schubfach mit gerundeter
Front von Leicht.

Drawer with unit for
cutlery by Leicht.

*Tiroir avec élément pour
couverts de chez Leicht.*

Schublade mit
Besteckmodul von Leicht.

Bottle rack unit with
pull-out tray by Leicht.

*Élément pour bouteilles
avec plateau escamotable
de chez Leicht.*

Flaschenmodul mit
herausziehbares Tablett
von Leicht.

Unit with double pull-out
shelf by Alno.

*Élément avec double
étagère escamotable
de chez Alno.*

Modul mit doppeltem,
herausziehbares
Regalbrett von Alno.

Recycling unit in work island by Leicht.

*Élément de recyclage dans une île centrale
de travail de chez Leicht.*

Recyclingmodul in Arbeitsinsel von Leicht.

Multi-purpose pull-out
unit by Mobalpa.

*Élément polyvalent
escamotable de chez Mopalpa.*

Verschiedenartig nutzbares,
herausziehbares Modul
von Mobalpa.

Unit with two shelves and two trays by Mobalpa.

Élément avec deux étagères et deux plateaux de chez Mobalpa.

Modul mit zwei Regalbrettern und zwei Tabletts von Mobalpa.

Detail of unit by Leicht.

*Détail d'un élément
de chez Leicht.*

Detailansicht eines
Moduls von Leicht.

Organizer unit
by Tielsa.

*Élément de rangement
de chez Tielsa.*

Organisatormodul
von Tielsa.

Organizer unit
with sliding tray
by Tielsa.

*Élément de rangement
avec plateau coulissant
de chez Tielsa.*

Organisatormodul
mit verschiebbaren
Tablett von Tielsa.

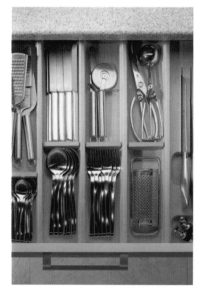

Unit for cutlery and knives by Leicht.

Élément pour couverts et couteaux de chez Leicht.

Modul für Besteck und Messer von Leicht.

| Diverse organizer systems by Alno. | *Divers systèmes de rangement de chez Alno.* | Verschiedene Systeme für Organisatoren von Alno. |

Below sink unit with recycling
bin by Flipper.

*Élément au-dessous un évier
avec poubelle de recyclage
de chez Flipper.*

Modul unter Spüle mit
Recyclingbehälter von Flipper.

Small unit for
spices by Alno.

*Petit élément pour épices
de chez Alno.*

Kleines Modul für
Gewürze von Alno.

Cutlery unit
by Nolte.

*Élément pour couverts
de chez Nolte.*

Besteckmodul
von Nolte.

Unit for utensils and
knife by Nolte.

*Élément pour ustensiles et
couteaux de chez Nolte.*

Modul für Utensilien und
Messer von Nolte.

Adjustable divider
unit by Nolte.

*Élément avec séparation
réglable de chez Nolte.*

Modul mit regulierbaren
Separator von Nolte.

Double width drawer
with dividers by Poggen.

*Tiroir extra large
avec séparations
de chez Poggen.*

Doppelte,breite
Schublade mit
Separatoren von Poggen.

Mobalpa kitchen
Sarila model.

*Cuisine Mobalpa
mod. Sarila.*

Küche Mobalpa
Modell Sarila.

Organizer units by
Mobalpa.

*Élément de rangement
de chez Mobalpa.*

Organisatormodul
von Mobalpa.

Organizer units
by Poggen.

*Élément de rangement
de chez Poggen.*

Organisatormodule
von Poggen.

Larder   *Les gardes-manger*   Speisekammer

Long-term conservation foods are kept in built-in storage units with double doors, sometimes with racks on the inside face to make maximum use of the available space and not lose the least used products. The pharmacy-style pull-out units are organized in diverse heights by means of aluminum racks so that they can also be used as bottle racks, taking advantage of narrow spaces which would otherwise remain under-used.

Les aliments de longue conservation sont habituellement gardés dans des alcôves encastrées à double porte, parfois en grillage dans la partie intérieure afin de profiter au maximum l'espace disponible et ne pas périmer les produits les moins utilisés. Les élément escamotables style armoires à pharmacie sont placés à différentes hauteurs grâce à des grillages en aluminium qui permettent de ranger des bouteilles tout en profitant de tous les petits espaces non utilisés.

Lang haltbare Lebensmittel werden in eingebauten Speiseschränken mit doppelter Tür aufbewahrt. Diese manchmal im Inneren mit Gitter versehenen Schränke dienen der maximalen Ausnützung des verfügbaren Platzes und verhindern das Verlieren von selten benützten Produkten. Herausziehbare Module im Stile einer Apotheke, planen in verschiedenen Höhen mittels Aluminiumgitter die Aufbewahrung, zum Teil auch als Flaschenhalter und nützen so Räume, die sonst nicht ausgelastet wären.

Previous page:
Pull out larder unit by Alno.

Page précédents:
Élément garde-manger
escamotable de chez Alno.

Auf der vorherigen Seite:
Herausziehbares Speisemodul
von Alno.

Organizer for jars and
auxiliary items by Alno.

Rangement pour pots et
auxiliaires de chez Alno.

Organisator für Einmachgläser
und Hilfsmittel von Alno.

Cabinet unit with
grille shelves by Alno.

*Élément garde-manger
avec étagères en grillage
de chez Alno.*

Speisemodul mit
Gitterregalen von Alno.

Corner larder
unit by Alno.

*Élément garde-manger
en coin de chez Alno.*

Eckspeisemodul von Alno.

Multi-purpose unit with 4
shelves by Alno.

*Élément polyvalent de 4
étagères de chez Alno.*

Verschiedenartig nützbares
Modul mit vier
Regalbrettern von Alno.

False bottomed
unit by Alno.

*Élément garde-manger à
double fond de chez Alno.*

Speisemodul mit doppelter
Rückwand von Alno.

Unit with double drawer and
chopping board by Alno.

*Élément avec double compartiment
et table à couper de chez Alno.*

Modul mit doppeltem Schubfach
und Schneidebrett von Alno.

Pull-out unit with
panel door by Alno.

*Élément escamotable avec
porte revêtue de chez Alno.*

Herausziehbares Modul mit
Relieffür Tür von Alno.

Wicker drawers for fresh
produce by Leicht.

*Tiroirs en osier pour produits
frais de chez Leicht.*

Korbschubladen für frische
Produkte von Leicht.

Wicker drawers with
handles by Alno.

*Tiroirs en osier avec
manettes de chez Alno.*

Korbschubladen mit
Griffen von Alno.

Wicker drawers with
handles by Alno.

*Tiroirs en osier avec
manettes de chez Alno.*

**Korbschubladen mit
Griffen von Alno.**

Unit with baskets and
trays by Alno.

*Élément avec paniers et
plateaux de chez Alno.*

**Modul mit Körben und
Tabletts von Alno.**

Units for packaged foods and vegetables by Alno.	*Éléments pour pots et féculents de chez Alno.*	**Modul für Verpacktes und Gemüse von Alno.**

Larder with fitted shelves
by Alno

*Garde-manger avec étagère
face à face de chez Alno*

Speisekammer mit
Regalen von Alno

Recycling unit
by Tielsa.

*Élément pour recyclage
de chez Tielsa.*

Recyclingmodul
von Tielsa.

Triple shelf unit by Leicht.

*Élément avec triple
étagère de chez Leicht.*

Modul mit drei Regalbrettern
von Leicht.

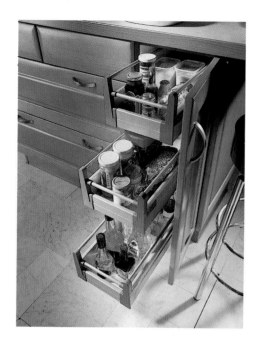

Corner larder
unit with fitted
shelves by Mobalpa.

*Élément garde-manger en
coin avec étagères face à
face de chez Mobalpa.*

Eckspeisemodul
mit Regalbrettern
von Mobalpa.

Pull-out triple drawer
unit by Alno.

*Élément avec triple tiroir
escamotable de chez Alno.*

Modul mit drei
herausziehbaren
Schubladen von Alno.

False bottomed
unit by Poggen.

*Élément avec double fond
de chez Poggen.*

Modul mit doppelter
Rückwand von Poggen.

Lighting / *L'Éclairage*
Beleuchtung

Good lighting must take account of the wholes space as well as the work areas and counter space. Both general lighting and spotlights can be either recessed or freestanding. Neon or fluorescent lighting consume less energy and last longer, while halogens are good for work areas and as back-ups in extractor hoods. Lamps of industrial design have been introduced as general (ambience) lighting. It should be borne in mind that spotlights plus general lighting cast shadows that can create undesirable effects in a space designed to be aseptic.

Un bon éclairage doit considérer la totalité de l'espace et de la superficie des différents plans de travail. On peut choisir des spots encastrés ou des lampes de tous genres autant pour un éclairage général comme pour un coin en particulier. Les néons ou fluorescents consomment très peu d'énergie et durent plus longtemps pendant que les halogènes sont recommandées pour les plans de travail et comme apport de lumière pour la hotte extracteur. Le dernier cri consiste à utiliser des lampes de design industriel comme éclairage d'ambiance. Il ne faut pas oublier que la somme d'un éclairage ponctuel et général provoquent des clairs-obscurs très désagréable dans une pièce créée pour avoir l'aspect le plus net possible.

Eine gute Beleuchtung muß den gesamten Raum und die Arbeitsbereiche über der Arbeitsplatte berücksichtigen. Für das Gesamtlicht genauso wie für das punktuelle Licht kann man zwischen eingebauten Lichtern (Strahlern) und freien Lichtern (Lampen) wählen. Neon- oder Leuchtstoffröhren haben einen geringen Stromverbrauch und eine lange Lebensdauer, während die Halogenlampen im Arbeitsbereich und als Unterstützungslichter in der Dunstabzugshaube ihre Vorteile haben. In letzter Zeit sieht man auch Lampen im industriellen Design als Gesamtlicht. Vergessen Sie nicht, daB die Summe aus punktuellem und Gesamtlicht ein Licht- und Schattengemisch ergibt, welches unangenehme Effekte in einem als antiseptisch entworfenen Raum schaffen kann.

Previous page:
Alno halogen spotlight.

Page. Précédente:
Spot halogène
de chez Alno.

Auf der vorherigen Seite:
Halogenstrahler von Alno.

Alno lamps beneath a shelf with incorporated sockets.

Lampe au-dessous d'un placard
de chez Alno.

Lampen unter Schrank mit
Stromabnehmern von Alno.

Alno lamp beneath
a shelf.

*Lampe au-dessous d'un
placard de chez Alno.*

**Lampe unter Schrank
von Alno.**

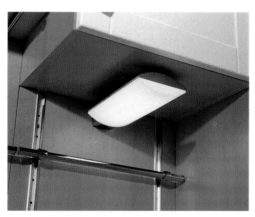

Alno neon lamp.

*Lampe en néon
de chez Alno.*

**Neonleuchte
von Alno.**

Alno halogen spotlight
with socket.

*Spot halogène avec prise
de courrant de chez Alno.*

**Halogenstrahler mit
Steckdose von Alno.**

Alno halogen lamps.

*Série de 2 lampes
halogène de chez alno.*

Serie aus zwei
Halogenlampen
von Alno.

Alno halogen lamps.

*Série de 3 lampes
halogènes de chez Alno.*

Serie aus 3
Halogenlampen
von Alno.

Casawell lighted cases.

*Vitrine avec éclairage
intérieur de chez Casawell.*

Vitrinen mit
Innenbeleuchtung
von Casawell.

Martinica neon tube
beneath a cabinet.

*Tube en néon au-dessous
d'un placard de chez
Martinica.*

Neonröhre unter
Schrank von Martinica.

Tielsa lighted cases.

Vitrines avec éclairage intérieur de chez Tielsa.

Vitrinen mit
Innenbeleuchtung
von Tielsa.

Casawell lighted cases.

Vitrine avec éclairage intérieur de chez Casawell.

Vitrine mit
Innenbeleuchtung
von Casawell.

Giamaica recessed
spotlights beneath
a cabinet.

*Extracteur
avec halogène
de chez Giamaica.*

Dunstabzug mit
Halogenlampe
von Giamaica.

Detail of Giamaica
halogen spotlights in a
decorative extractor.

*Détail de spot halogène
pou extracteur décoratif
de chez Giamaica.*

Detailansicht von
Halogenstrahlern für
dekorativen Dunstabzug
von Giamaica.

Giamaica halogen
spotlights in a
decorative extractor.

*Halogènes encastrés
au-dessous d'un placard
de chez Giamaica.*

Eingebaute
Halogenlampen unter
Schrank von Giamaica.

Mobalpa lighted cases.

Vitrines avec éclairage intérieur de chez Mobalpa.

Vitrinen mit Innenbeleuchtung von Mobalpa.

Mobalpa halogen lamps.

Lampes halogènes de chez Mobalpa.

Halogenlampen von Mobalpa.

Neon tube beneath Martinica cabinet.

Tube en néon au-dessous d'un placard de chez Martinica.

Neonröhre unter Schrank von Martinica.

Febal Lemon model decorative
extractor hood.

*Hotte décorative mod. Lemon
de chez Febal.*

Dekorativer Dunstabzug
Modell Lemon von Febal.

Nolte Lido model
decorative extractor hood.

*Hotte décorative mod.
Lido de chez Nolte.*

Dekorativer Dunstabzug
Modell Lido von Nolte.

Mobalpa decorative
extractor hood.

*Hotte décorative
de chez Mobalpa.*

Dekorativer Dunstabzug
von Mobalpa.

Nolte Milano model
decorative extractor hood.

*Hotte décorative mod.
Milano de chez Nolte.*

Dekorative
Dunstabzugshaube Modell
Milano von Nolte.

Halogen lamps
beneath Nolde
Life model.

*Halogène au-dessous
d'un placard mod.
Life de chez Nolte.*

Halogenlampen unter
Schrank Modell Life
von Nolte.

Spotlights over Nolde
Dallas model cabinet.

*Spots au-dessus d'un
plan de travail mod.
Dallas de chez Nolte.*

Strahler über
Arbeitsplatte Modell
Dallas von Nolte.

Halogens beneath Nobilia
Natura model cabinet.

*Halogènes au-dessous d'un placard
mod. Natura de chez Nobilia.*

Halogenlampen unter Schrank
Model Natura von Nobilia.

Nolte Lineade
model halogens.

Halogènes mod.
Linea de chez
Nolte.

Halogenlampen
Modell Linea
von Nolte.

Spotlights beneath
Nolte Ravenna
model cabinet.

*Spots au-dessous
d'un placard mod.
Ravenne de chez
Nolte.*

Strahler unter
Schrank Modell
Ravenna von
Nolte.

Sarila Brat model
lighted case.

*Vitrine avec
éclairage intérieur
mod. Brat
de chez Sarila.*

Vitrine mit
Innenbeleuchtung
Modell Brat
von Sarila.

Nolte Lago model halogens.

Halogènes mod. Lago de chez Nolte.

Halogenlampen Modell Lago von Nolte.

Spotlights beneath Nobilia Orion model cabinet.

Spots au-dessous d'un placard mod. Orion de chez Nobilia.

Strahler unter Schrank Modell Orion von Nobilia.

Halogens beneath Nobilia Pia
model cabinets.

*Halogène au-dessus d'un
placard mod. Pia
de chez Nobilia.*

Halogenlampen über
Schrank Modell Pia
von Nobilia.

Febal Playa model.

Mod. Playa de chez Febal.

Modell Playa von Febal.

Mobalpa modules with interior lighting.

Élément avec éclairage intérieur de chez Mobalpa.

Module mit Innenbeleuchtung von Mobalpa.

Mobalpa Orade model lamps.

Lampes mod. Ora de chez Mobalpa.

Lampen Model Orade von Mobalpa.

Nobilia Tivolide model
halogen series.

*Série d'halogènes mod. Tivoli
de chez Nobilia.*

Serie aus Halogenlampen
Modell Tivolide von Nobilia.

Nobilia Pia model.

Mod. Pia de chez Nobilia.

Modell Pia von Nobilia.

Nolte original model.

Original modèle de chez Nolte.

Originelles Modell von Nolte.

Nobilia Orion model skylight.

Éclairage général mod. Orion de chez Nobilia.

Zenitlicht Modell Orion von Nobilia.

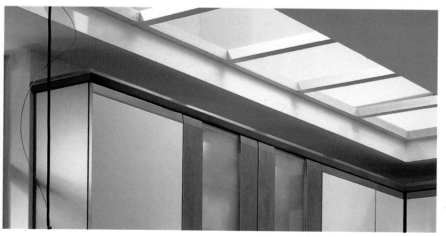

Areas of the kitchen / *Les différents plans de cuisine*
Bereiche in der Küche

The kitchen is divided into three main areas: preparation, cooking and washing, while storage is distributed on all fronts, whether in upper, lower or additional closets. Currently, there is a tendency to include an eating area in the kitchen. The size varies according to the needs of each family, sometimes joining two rooms in one. The principles of ergonomics recommend that the distribution of the different areas follow the natural flow of work to save on superfluous movements which could result in fatigue.

La cuisine est divisée en trois espaces principaux : préparation, cuisson et lavage, alors que le rangement est réparti un peu partout dans les placards supérieurs, inférieurs ou annexés. Actuellement on a tendance à inclure dans les cuisines un office pour les repas dont les dimensions varient selon les besoins de chaque familles en assemblant parfois deux pièces en une seule. Selon les principes de l'ergonomie, il est conseillé d'organiser les différents plans de travail selon leur séquence naturelle pour éviter des mouvements superflus qui peuvent provoquer de la fatigue.

Die Küche teilt sich in drei Hauptzonen auf: Vorbereitung, Kochen und Waschen, während die Aufbewahrung auf die gesamten Fronten verteilt wird, gleichermaBen auf Hängeschränke wie auf Unterschränke oder auf angebaute Module. In letzter Zeit geht man wieder dazu über in die Küche einen Essbereich einzuschlieBen, welcher in seiner GröBe je nach Familienbedürfniss variiert, und der machmal auch zwei Zimmer verbindet. Die Prinzipien der Ergonomie raten uns, die verschiedenen Bereiche so aufzuteilen, daB sie der natürlichen Arbeitssequenz folgen, um überflüssige, ermüdende Bewegungen einzusparen.

Miele kitchen with glass and aluminum table.

Cuisine Miele avec table en verre et aluminium.

Mieleküche mit Aluminiumglastisch.

Preparation *La préparation* Vorbereitung

Current kitchens consist of closet units which run the length of the wall, with the counter top being the area devoted to preparation. It is normally situated in the spaces left free by the cooking and washing area. The work surface must be made of an easy to clean material, with a predominance of natural materials: wood, marble, granite and the solid competence of synthetic materials which triumph because of their versatility, as well as steel, adopted from professional kitchens.

Les cuisines actuelles se composent de placards modulaires qui suivent la ligne du mur et le plan de travail devient l'endroit destiné à la préparation des aliments. Celle-ci est normalement situé entre l'espace destiné au lavage et celui destiné à la cuisson. Ce plan de travail est fait habituellement avec un matériel facile à nettoyer, et très souvent naturel: bois-, marbre, granite mais aussi les synthétiques qui triomphent grâce à leur versatilité ainsi que l'acier adapté aux cuisines professionnelles.

Die aktuellen Küchen setzen sich aus Schrankmodulen zusammen, die der Länge der Wand folgen, wobei die Arbeitsplatte der für Vorbereitungen vorgesehene Bereich ist, welcher normalerweise neben den für Waschen und Kochen vorgesehenen Bereichen liegt. Die Oberfläche des Arbeitsbereichs muß aus leicht zu reinigendem Material sein, bevorzugt werden natürliche Stoffe wie Holz, Marmor, Granit aber auch die sehr wettbewerbsfähigen synthetischen Stoffe, welche durch ihre Flexibilität bestechen, oder Stahl, der ursprünglich aus der profesionellen Küchen kommt.

Previous page:
Display case between units with 3 sockets by Miele.

Page précédente:
Vitrine entre éléments avec 3 prises de courant de chez Miele.

Auf der vorherigen Seite:
Vitrine zwischen Modulen mit 3 Stromabnehmern von Miele.

Display case with sliding door and collapsible overhead cabinets by Miele.

rine avec porte coulissante et placard supérieur abattable de chez Miele.

Vitrine mit Schiebetür und oberen nterklappbaren Schränken von Miele.

Overhanging
counter top
with curved profile
and synthetic
surface by Leicht.

*Plan de travail avec
prolongement et
profil arrondi, et
dessus synthétique
de chez Leicht.*

Arbeitsplatte mit
gerundeten Profil
und synthetischer
Oberfläche von Leicht.

Unit with shutter closure with
slide-in knife storage by Poggen.

*Élément avec fermeture à volets
et orifices pour couteaux
de chez Poggen.*

Modul mit Jalousieverschluß
und Schlitzen für Messer
von Poggen.

Set of two-colored
units by Leicht.

*Ensemble d'éléments
bicolore de chez Leicht*

Ensemble aus zweifarbigen
Modulen von Leicht.

Preparation area of the
model Le Foglie by Florida.

*Coin de préparation du
mod. Le Foglie de chez Florida.*

Vorbereitungsbereich des
Modells Le Foglie von Florida.

Circular unit with
wooden counter top model
Milano 781 by Nolte.

*Modèle circulaire avec plan
de travail en bois mod. Milano
781 de chez Nolte.*

Kreisförmiges Modell mit
Arbeitsplatte aus Holz Modell
Milano 781 von Nolte.

White sink with sliding
chopping board by Nolte.

*Évier blanc avec table à couper
coulissante de chez Nolte.*

Weiße Spüle mit verschiebbarer
Schneideplatte von Nolte.

Kitchen front
model Venus by Florida.

*Front de cuisine mod. Venus
de chez Florida*

Küchenfront
Modell Venus von Florida.

Two-colored work
peninsul by Alno.

*Presqu'île de travail
bicolore de chez Alno.*

Zweifarbige
Arbeitshalbinsel von Alno.

Preparation island with
series of drawers by Alno.

*Île de préparation avec
série de tiroirs de chez Alno.*

Vorbereitungsinsel mit
Schubladenserie von Alno.

Central work island by Alno.

Île de travail centrale de chez Alno.

Zentrale Arbeitsinsel von Alno.

Cooking front with
folding table by Alno.

*Front de cuisson avec
table pliable de chez Alno.*

Kochfront mit
zusammmenklappbaren
Tisch von Alno.

Laminated kitchen
in white by Alno.

*Cuisine revêtue en blanc
de chez Alno.*

Weiß furnierte
Küche von Alno.

Extensible table
model Trendy by Florida.

*Table extensible mod. Trendy
de chez Florida.*

Ausziehtisch
Modell Trendy von Florida.

U-shaped kitchen
by Alno.

*Cuisine en forme de U
de chez Alno*

Küche in U-Form
von Alno.

Central work unit model
Cortina by Nobilia.

*Élément de travail central
mod. Cortina de chez Nobilia.*

**Zentrales Arbeitsmodul
Modell Cortina von Nobilia.**

Unit with wheels
model Cosmo by Nobilia.

*Élément sur roues mod.
Cosmo de chez Nobilia.*

**Modul mit Rädern
Modell Cosmo von Nobilia.**

Work island with attached
eating table model Ravenna
853 by Nolte.

*Île de travail avec table à repas
adossée mod. Ravenna 853
de chez Nolte.*

**Arbeitsinsel mit angebautem
Esstisch Modell Ravenna 853
von Nolte.**

Cooking island with dining bar
model Flair by Nolte.

*Île de cuisson avec barre pour repas
mod. Flair de chez Nolte.*

**Kochinsel mit Esstheke Modell
Flair von Nolte.**

Large washing and preparation
island with raised breakfast bar
model Milano 781 by Nolte.

*Grande île de lavage et préparation
avec barre élevée pour petits déjeuners
mod. Milano 781 de chez Nolte.*

GroBe Wasch- und
Vorbereitungsinsel mit hoher
Frühstückstheke
Modell Milano 781 von Nolte.

Washing   *Le lavage*   Waschen

The washing area is usually situated below a window to make the task less tedious, although the current trend is to skip these rules to present washing islands or peninsulas which capture all the visual attention in this task. Sinks are manufactured in stainless steel and porcelain with an ever increasing use of synthetic materials which perfectly imitate traditional ones in rustic and classical models. The most sophisticated models have rinsing trays or sloping draining boards with drainage and fluting to fit the chopping board.

Le coin de lavage se situe habituellement au-dessous de la fenêtre pour rendre la tache plus distrayante, bien que la tendance actuelle fuit des normes établies pour présenter des îles et des presqu'îles de lavage qui attraient toute notre attention. Les éviers sont réalisés en acier inoxydable et porcelaine avec une tendance de plus en plus marquée pour les matériaux synthétiques qui imitent de mieux en mieux les modèles rustiques et classiques traditionnels. Les modèles les plus sophistiqués sont réalisés avec des plateaux pour rincer ou de égouttoirs inclinés avec un égout et des stries pour encastrer la table à couper.

Der Waschbereich ist normalerweise unter einem Fenster angesiedelt, um die Arbeit wenig ärgerlich zu machen, obwohl aktuelle Tendenzen diese Norm verletzen, um Waschinseln oder Halbinseln zu präsentieren, welche die ganze visuelle Aufmerksamkeit dieser Arbeit einfangen. Die Spülbecken werden aus rostfreiem Stahl und Porzelan fabriziert, wobei der Anteil an synthetischen Materialien jedes mal größer ist, da diese die traditionellen der klassischen und rustikalen Modelle perfekt immitieren. Die am höchsten entwickelten Modelle haben Tabletts zum Auspülen, angeschrägte Abtropfeinrichtungen mit Abfluß oder Rillen um Schneidebretter einzupassen.

Previous page:
Washing island with two bowl model Lof by Mobalpa-Sarila.

Page précédente:
Île de lavage avec deux bacs mod. Lof de chez Mobalpa-Sarila.

Auf der vorherigen Seite:
Waschinsel mit zwei Spülbeckem Modell Lof von Mobalpa-Sarila.

Single bowl stainless steel sink with draining board and chopping board by Casawell.

Évier en acier inoxydable d'un bac avec égouttoir et table à couper de chez Casawell.

Spüle aus rostfreiem Stahl mit einer Vertiefung, Abtropfgestell und Schneideplatte von Casawell.

Stainless steel sink and rear
shelf with orifices by
Martinica.

*Évier en acier inoxydable et
étagère postérieure avec
orifices de chez Martinica.*

Spüle aus rostfreiem Stahl,
nachgelagerte Konsole mit
Vertiefungen von Martinica.

Two-bowl stainless steel sink
with mixer tap by Alno.

*Évier en acier inoxydable avec deux bacs et
robinet tuyau d'arrosage de chez Alno.*

Spüle aus rostfreiem Stahl mit zwei
Becken und Schlauchgriff von Alno.

Single bowl sink with
washing tray and
draining board with drainage by Alno.

*Évier d'un bac avec plateau pour lavage
,égouttoir et égout de chez Alno.*

Spüle mit einer Vertiefung,
Fläche zum Waschen und
Abtropfbereich mit Abfluß von Alno.

Stainless steel sink model
Mixer 2000 by Florida.

*Évier en acier inoxydable
mod. Mixer 2000
de chez Florida.*

Spüle aus rostfreiem
Stahl Modell Mixer 2000
von Florida.

Peninsula with two-bowl sink model Everg by Febal.	*Presqu'île avec évier de deux bacs mod. Everg de chez Febal.*	Halbinsel mit Spüle mit zwei Becken Modell Everg von Febal.	Double basin stainless steel sink below synthetic counter top by Elledue/House.	*Évier en acier inoxydable de deux bacs au-dessous d'un plan de travail synthétique de chez Elledue\ House.*	Spüle aus rostfreiem Stahl mit zwei Becken und synthetischer Arbeitsplatte von Elledue/House.

Curved sink with rear
draining board
by Leicht.

*Évier arrondi avec
égouttoir postérieur
de chez Leicht.*

Gerundete Spüle
mit nachgelagertem
Abtropfgestell
von Leicht.

Two-bowl sink in synthetic
material model Sintesi
by Florida.

*Évier de deux bacs en matériel
synthétique mod. Sintesi
de chez Florida.*

Spüle mit zwei Becken aus
synthetischem Material
Modell Sintesi von Florida.

Washing peninsula with
sliding chopping board
by Leicht.

*Presqu'île de lavage avec
table à couper coulissante
de chez Leicht*

Waschhalbinsel mit
verschiebbarem
Schneidebrett von Leicht.

Alsa rustic sink
by Leicht.

*Évier rustique Alsa
de chez Leicht*

**Rustikale Spüle Modell
Alsa von Leicht.**

Previous page:
Stainless steel sink with
draining board and slot-in
chopping board model Old
Style by Florida.

*Page précédente:
Évier en acier inoxydable
avec plateau égouttoir et
table à couper encastrée
mod. Old Style de chez
Florida.*

Auf der vorherigen Seite:
Spüle aus rostfreiem Stahl
mit Abtropffläche und
eingepasstem
Schneidebrett Modell Old
Style von Florida.

Peninsula with
embedded sink model
Flora by Febal.

*Presqu'île avec évier
incrusté mod. Flora
de chez Febal.*

Halbinsel mit
Spüle Modell Flora
von Febal.

Dual sink for
corners by Mobalpa.

*Évier de deux bacs pour un
angle de chez Mobalpa.*

Ecspüle mit zwei
Vertiefungen von Mobalpa.

Round stainless steel
sink by Nolte.

*Évier arrondi en acier
inoxydable de chez Nolte.*

Runde Spüle aus
rostfreiem Stahl von Nolte.

Stainless steel sink with draining
board by Mobalpa.

*Évier en acier inoxydable avec
égouttoir de chez Mobalpa.*

Spüle aus rostfreiem Stahl mit
Abtropfläche von Mobalpa.

Butterfly wing stainless steel
sink by Nolte.

*Évier en aile de papillon et acier
inoxydable de chez Nolte.*

Spüle "Schmetterlingsflügel"
aus rostfreiem Stahl von Nolte.

Ergonomic model
sink by Nolte.

*Évier mod. Ergonomie
de chez Nolte.*

Spüle Modell Ergonomie
von Nolte.

Dual sink in work island
model Lof by Mobalpa-Sarila.

*Évier de deux bacs incrusté
dans une île de travail mod.
Lof de chez Mobalpa-Sarila.*

Inkrustierte Spüle mit
zwei Vertiefungen in
Arbeitsinsel Modell Lof
von Mobalpa-Sarila.

Sink Brat model
by Mobalpa.

*Évier mod. Brat
de chez Mobalpa.*

Spüle Modell Brat
von Mobalpa.

Single bowl stainless
steel sink by Casawell.

*Évier d'un bac en acier
inoxydable de chez Casawell.*

Spülee mit einer Vertiefung
aus rostfreiem Stahl
von Casawell.

Sink in synthetic material
model Ora by Mobalpa.

*Évier en matière synthétique
mod. Ora de chez Mobalpa.*

Spüle aus synthetischem Material
Modell Ora von Mobalpa.

Sink with garbage disposal
unit model Tos by Mobalpa.

*Evier avec appareil à triturer
mod. Tos de chez Mobalpa.*

Spüle mit
Zerkleinerungsmaschine
Modell Tos von Mobalpa.

Extra-long sink by Alno.

Évier extra large de chez Alno.

Extralange Spüle von Alno.

Rustic style white sink
by Mobalpa.

*Évier blanc style rustique
de chez Mobalpa.*

Weiße Spüle im rustikalen
Stil von Mobalpa.

Cooking — *La cuisson* — Kochen

The latest models favor the omnipresence of ceramic or induction hobs with irregular shapes, planned for the needs of their users. Ovens are presented in a continuous front with the hob or built into a column at medium height, together with the now indispensable microwave. The extractor hood becomes a decorative element which highlights its essential function in the most up-to-date kitchen.

Les plaques de cuisson vitrocéramiques ou d'induction sont devenues omniprésentes et la plupart des modèles ont une forme irrégulière pour satisfaire les besoins des éventuels clients. Les fours sont situés sur le même plan que la plaque de cuisson ou en colonne à mi-hauteur à coté de l'incontournable microonde. La hotte extracteur est devenue un élément décoratif qui rehausse sa fonction essentielle dans la cuisine actuelle.

Die aktuellen Modelle entscheiden sich für die Allgegenwart der Glaskeramik- oder Induktionskochfelder, mit unregelmäßigen Formen, gedacht für die verschiedenen Bedürfnisse der eventuellen Benutzer. Die Öfen präsentieren sich in ununterbrochener Front mit dem Kochfeld oder auch eingebaut in einer Säule auf halber Höhe neben dem heutzutage unumgänglichen Mikrowellenherd. Die Dunstabzugshaube verwandelt sich zu einem dekorativen Element, das seine wesentliche Funktion in der aktuellen Küche unterstreicht.

Previous page:
Professional cooking unit model
Lof by Mobalpa.

Page précédente:
Élément de cuisson professionnel
mod. Lof de chez Mobalpa.

Auf der vorherigen Seite:
Professionelles Kochmodul
Modell Lof von Mobalpa.

Cooking hob with extractor by Miele.

Plaque de cuisson avec extracteur
de chez Miele.

Kochfeld mit Dunstabzugshaube
von Miele.

Ceramic hob by Leicht.

Plaque vitrocéramique de chez Leicht.

Glaskeramikkochfeld von Leicht.

Cooking front with extractor by Leicht.

Plan de cuisson avec extracteur de chez Leicht.

Kochfront mit Dunstabzgshaube von Leicht.

Cooking hob with 4 rings by Leicht.

Plaque de cuisson de 4 feux de chez Leicht.

Kochfeld mit vier Kochstellen von Leicht.

Cooking unit with wooden
front by Leicht.

*Élément de cuisson avec
front en bois de chez Leicht.*

**Kochmodul mit Holzfront
von Leicht.**

Hob for one ring
by Siemens.

*Plaque pour un feu
de chez Siemens.*

**Kochplatte für eine
Kochstelle von Siemens.**

Cooking hob with oven
by Whirlpool.

*Plaque de cuisson avec
four de chez Whirlpool.*

**Kochfeld mit Ofen
von Whirlpool.**

Cooking hob for 3
rings by Mobalpa.

*Plaque de cuisson pour 3 feux
de chez Mobalpa.*

Kochfeld für drei Kochstellen
von Mobalpa.

Gas burners and oven
by Mobalpa.

*Brûleur à gaz et four
de chez Mobalpa.*

Gasbrenner und Ofen
von Mobalpa.

Extra-long
cooking hob
by Alsa.

*Plaque de cuisson
extra large
de chez Alsa*

Extra langes
Kochfeld
von Alsa.

Cooking hob for gas
by Mobalpa.

*Plaque de cuisson pour gaz
de chez Mobalpa*

Kochfeld für Gas
von Mobalpa.

Cooking unit with
extractor by Siematic.

*Élément de cuisson avec
extracteur de chez Siematic.*

Kochmodul mit
Dunstabzugshaube
von Siematic.

Unit with cooking
hob and oven by Macro
Element.

*Élément avec plaque de
cuisson et four de Macro
Element.*

Modul mit Kochfeld und
Ofen von Macro Element.

Following page:
Unit with cooking
hob, oven and extractor.

*Page suivante:
Elément avec plaque de
cuisson, four et extracteur.*

Auf der folgenden Seite:
Modul mit Kochfeld, Ofen
und Dunstabzugshaube.

Ceramic hob and
extractor by Mobalpa.

*Plaque vitrocéramique et
extracteur de chez Mobalpa.*

Glaskeramikkochfeld und
Dunstabzug von Mobalpa.

Hob with 5 gas burners
model Mixer 2000
by Florida.

*Plaque avec 5 brûleurs
à gaz mod. Mixer 2000
de chez Florida.*

Kochfeld mit 5
Gaskochstellen Modell
Mixer 2000 von Florida.

Ceramic hob and
flat extractor by Mobalpa.

*Plaque vitrocéramique et
extracteur plat de chez
Mobalpa.*

Glaskeramikkochfeld und
Flache Dunstabzugshaube
von Mobalpa.

Cooking front with oven
and extractor by Siemens.

*Plan de cuisson avec four et
extracteur de chez Siemens.*

Kochfront mit Ofen und
Dunstabzug von Siemens.

Continuous cooking
front by Mobalpa.

*Plan de cuisson continu
de chez Mobalpa.*

Ununterbrochene
Kochfront von Mobalpa.

Professional kitchen
model Ora by Mobalpa.

*Cuisine professionnelle
mod. Ora de chez Mobalpa.*

Professionelle Küche
Modell Ora von Mobalpa.

Bathrooms
·
Les Salle de bain
·
Bäder

 Modern | *Les Modernes* | Moderne

 Rustic and Classic | *Les classiques et les rustiques*
Klassische und Rustikale

 Furniture | *Le Mobilier* | Möbel

 Sinks | *Les Lavabos* | Waschgelegenheiten

 Sanitary | *Les Sanitaires* | Toiletten

 Accessories | *Les Accessoires* | Zubehör

 Faucets | *Le Robineterie* | Armaturen

 Bathtubs | *Les Baignoires* | Badewannen

 Showers | *Les Douches* | Duschen

 Lighting | *L'Éclairage* | Beleuchtung

Modern / *Les modernes*
Moderne

The latest tendencies in bathrooms mark the triumph in straight-line furniture, the majority on legs, without very many references to past ages. On the other hand, daring is compensated by the traditional materials used (porcelain) in the sinks' unique low forms. And there is further compensation in the overall design, which converts the bath into a blend of the plain and the magnificent, a synthesis of one room in the house that takes on the function of health and beauty.

Les dernières tendances en salle de bain sont marquées par le triomphe de la ligne droite dans les meubles, la plus part sur pattes, sans trop recourir aux temps passés. Bien au contraire, l'audace est compensée par des matériaux traditionnels (porcelaine), représentés sous des formes curieuses dans les lavabos, de fait que la sophistication proposée converti la salle de bain en un mélange de sobriété et d'élégance, pour affirmer la synthèse d'une pièce de la maison devenu un véritable laboratoire de la santé ou un salon de beauté.

Die letzten Tendenzen im Badezimmer sind durch den Erfolg der geraden Linien bei den Möbeln gekennzeichnet, wobei diese meiBt auf FüBen stehen und anderen Epochen wenig Referenz erweisen. Im Gegensatz dazu wird diese Kühnheit mit traditionellen Materialien (Porzelan) ausgeglichen, welche in den Waschgelegenheiten in ausergewöhnlichen Formen präsentiert werden, und gekünstelten Angeboten, die das Badezimmer in einer Mischung von Schlichtheit und Würde in die Synthese eines Raumes zwischen Gesundheitslabor und Schönheitssalon verwandeln wollen.

Preceding page:
Duravit Vero model.

Page précédente:
Mod. Vero de chez Duravit.

Auf der vorherigen Seite:
Modell Vero von Duravit.

Porcelain bathroom ensembles.

Sanitaires en porcelaine dans
une ambiance rustique.

Sanitäre Einrichtungen aus
Porzelan in rustikaler Umgebung.

Raspel Euclide column sink.

*Lavabo en colonne Euclide
de chez Rapsel.*

Waschbeckensäule Euclide
von Rapsel.

Storch/Ehlers designs.

Deux design de chez Storch /Ehlers.

Entwürfe von Storch/Ehlers.

Storch/Ehlers designs.

Deux design de chez Storch /Ehlers.

Entwürfe von Storch/Ehlers.

Teo-Gaia/Elledue model.

Mod. Teo-Gaia de chez Elledue.

Modell Teo-Gaia von Elledue.

Roca Flash model.

Mod. Flash de chez Roca.

Modell Flash von Roca.

Teo-Gaia/Elledue
AE model.

*Mod. Teo-Gaia
de Elledue.*

Modell Teo-Gaia
von Elledue.

Teo-Gaia/Elledue AE model.

Modèle Teo-Gaia de chez Elledue.

Modell Teo-Gaia von Elledue.

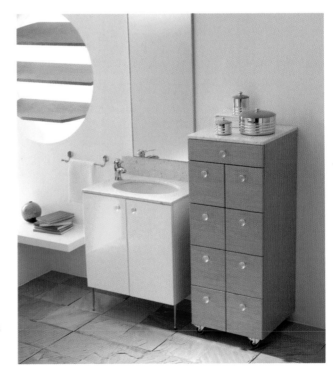

Next page:
Teo-Gaia/Elledue AE model.

Page précédente:
Modèle Teo-Gaia de chez Elledue.

Auf der nächsten Seite:
Modell Teo-Gaia von Elledue.

Roca Dama model.

Mod. Dama de chez Roca.

Modell Dama von Roca.

Previous page:
Villeroy Face-to-Face 1 model.

*Page précédente:
Mod. Face to Face 1
de chez Villeroy.*

Auf der vorherigen Seite:
Modell Face to face 1
von Villeroy.

Roca bathroom with two sinks.

*Salle de bain avec double lavabo
de chez Roca.*

Badezimmer mit doppeltem
Waschbecken von Roca,

Roca Sydney model.

Mod. Sydney de chez Roca.

Modell Dama von Roca.

Roca Meridian model.

Mod. Meridian de chez Roca.

Modell Meridian von Roca.

Roca Victoria model.

Mod. Victoria de chez Roca.

Modell Victoria von Roca.

Roca Giralda model.

Mod. Giralda de chez Roca.

Modell Giralda von Roca.

Roca Civic model.

Mod. Civic de chez Roca.

Modell Civic von Roca.

Roca Regata model.

Mod. Regata de chez Roca.

Modell Regata von Roca.

Duravit Multibox model.

*Mod. Multibox
de chez Duravit.*

Modell Multibox
von Duravit.

Copat Zodiaco series
model FS26.

*Mod. FS 26 de la série
Zodiaco de chez Copat.*

Modell FS26 aus der
Serie Zodiaco von Copat.

One of the models in the
Puris Style series.

Mod. Style de chez Puris.

Modell Style von Puris.

Elledue Teo-Gaia model .   *Mod. Teo-Gaia de chez Elledue.*   Modell Teo-Gaia von Elledue.

Elledue Teo-Gaia model.

*Mod. Teo-Gaia
de chez Elledue.*

Modell Teo-Gaia
von Elledue.

Villeroy Face-to-Face model.

Mod. Face to Face 2 de chez Villeroy.

Modell Face to face 2 von Villeroy.

Copat Zodiaco series,
model FS23.

*Mod. FS 23 de la série
Zodiaco de chez Copat.*

Modell FS23 aus der
Serie Zodiaco von Copat.

Zodiaco Elledue model.

*Modèles Zodiaco
de chez Elledue.*

Modell Zodiaco
von Elledue.

Elledue-Zodiaco
model FS40.

*Mod. FS 40 de la série
Zodiaco de chez Copat.*

Modell FS40 aus der
Serie Zodiaco von Copat.

Copat Zodiaco series,
model FS39.

*Mod. FS 39 de la série
Zodiaco de chez Copat.*

Modell FS39 aus der
Serie Zodiaco von Copat.

Elledue Zodiaco model.

*Mod. Zodiaco
de chez Elledue.*

Modell Zodiaco
von Elledue.

Previous page:
Elledue-Zodiaco model.

Page précédente:
Mod. Zodiaco
de chez Elledue.

Auf der vorherigen Seite:
Model Zodiaco
von Elledue.

Teo-Gaia/Elledue Serie.

Série Teo-Gaia de chez Elledue.

Serie Teo-Gaia von Elledue.

Next page:
Detail of Teo-Gaia/Elledue
modular series.

Page suivante:
Détail de la série modulaire
Teo-Gaia de chez Elledue.

Auf der folgenden Seite:
Detailansicht aus der Modulserie
Teo-Gaia von Elledue.

Detail of Teo-Gaia/Elledue
series.

*Détail de la série
Teo-Gaia de chez Elledue.*

Detailansicht aus der Serie
Teo-Gaia von Elledue.

Teo-Gaia/Elledue Serie.

Série Teo-Gaia de chez Elledue.

Serie Teo-Gaia von Elledue.

Variation of Teo-Gaia/Elledue model.

Variation du mod. Teo-Gaia de chez Elledue.

Abwandlung des Modells Teo-Gaia von Elledue.

Teo-Gaia/Elledue
Models.

*Modèles Teo-Gaia
de chez Elledue.*

Modell
Teo-Gaia von Elledue.

Teo-Gaia/Elledue Serie.

Série Teo-Gaia de chez Elledue.

Serie Teo-Gaia von Elledue.

Teo-Gaia/Elledue Models.   *Modèles Teo-Gaia de chez Elledue.*   **Modell Teo-Gaia von Elledue.**

Teo-Gaia
modular design.

*Design modulaire
Teo-Gaia de chez Elledue.*

Modulentwurf
Teo-Gaia von Elledue.

Teo-Gaia/Elledue
Models.

*Modèles Teo-Gaia
de chez Elledue.*

Modell
Teo-Gaia von Elledue.

Teo-Gaia/Elledue
Model.

*Modèle Teo-Gaia
de chez Elledue.*

Modell
Teo-Gaia von Elledue.

Variation of
Teo-Gaia/Elledue model.

*Série de salles de bain
Teo-Gaia de chez Elledue.*

Bäderserie
Teo-Gaia von Elledue.

Teo-Gaia/Elledue
model.

*Modèle Teo-Gaia
de chez Elledue.*

Modell Teo-Gaia
von Elledue.

Puris Natura model.

Mod. Natura de chez Puris.

Modell Natura von Puris.

Teo-Gaia/Elledue model.

*Modèle Teo-Gaia
de chez Elledue.*

Modell
Teo-Gaia von Elledue.

Laufen model.

Salle de bain de chez Laufen.

Bad von Laufen.

Teo-Gaia/Elledue model.

*Modèle Teo-Gaia
de chez Elledue.*

Modell
Teo-Gaia von Elledue.

Villeroy Nagano model.

Mod. Nagano de chez Villeroy.

Modell Nagano von Villeroy.

411

Tulli Ondula model.

Mod. Ondula de chez Tulli.

Modell Ondula von Tulli.

Tulli Tesi model.

Mod. Tesi de chez Tulli.

Modell Tesi von Tulli.

Tulli Ondula model.

Mod. Ondula de chez Tulli.

Modell Ondula von Tulli.

Tulli Quadri model.

Mod. Quadri de chez Tulli.

Modell Quadri von Tulli.

Tulli Quadri model.

Mod. Quadri de chez Tulli.

Modell Quadri von Tulli.

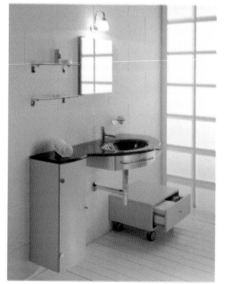

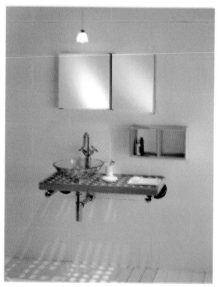

Villeroy Pure Basic model.   *Mod. Pure Basic de chez Villeroy.*   Modell Pure Basic von Villeroy.

Villeroy Pure Basic model.

Mod. Pure Basic de chez Villeroy.

Modell Pure Basic von Villeroy.

Villeroy Pure Basic model.

Mod. Pure Basic de chez Villeroy.

Modell Pure Basic von Villeroy.

Classical and Rustic / *Les classiques et les rustiques*
Klassische und Rustikale

Wood, porcelain, and marble are privileged materials. If the rustic variation prefers rudeness of form, solid pieces, and stunning finishes, the classical variation opts for lightness. The furniture has narrow legs, moldings, and curved forms in the basins. There are no apparent homages but rather a will to timelessness, a quality that never goes out of style, an attempt to establish sure values in taste. The bathroom is more of a boudoir than an aesthetician's clinic, providing to by accessories, with drawers for a thousand secrets, etched glass, and tubs without legs.

Le bois, la porcelaine et le marbre sont des matériaux privilégiés. Si les rustiques préfèrent les formes rudes, les pièces massives et les finitions vigoureuses, les classiques sont plutôt plus légères. Les pattes des meubles de lavabos sont plus étroites, en relief et avec des formes arrondies dans les cavités. On ne peut pas rendre hommage à une époque déterminée sans un désir d'intemporalité, qualité qui ne se démode pas tout en parient pour le goût pour les valeurs sures. La salle de bain tient plus du boudoir que de la clinique de chirurgie esthétique, grâce aux meubles auxiliaires plein de tiroirs secrets, les vitrines gravées à la cire, et les baignoires sur pattes.

Holz, Porzelan und Marmor sind die privilegierten Materialien. Obgleich die rustikale Variante die groben Formen, Massivholzteile und schlagkräftige Ausfertigungen bevorzugt, die klassische präsentiert sich eher leichter. Die Möbel haben schmalere Füße, Reliefe und gerundete Formen in den Freiräumen für das Waschbecken. Es gibt keine offensichtlichen Huldigunge andreuer Epochen, sondern eine freiwillige Zeitlosigkeit, eine Qualität die nicht im Modetrend vergeht, ein Setzen auf die sicheren Werte des Geschmacks. Das Badezimmer hat mehr von einem Boudoir als von einer Schöhnheitsklinik, was sich in den zusätzlichen Möbeln, den Schubladen für tausend Geheimnisse, dem gravierten Glas oder den freistehenden Badewannen mit Füßen fortsetzt.

Previous page:
Elledue Plaza series.

Page précédente:
Série Plaza de chez
Elledue.

Auf der vorherigen Seite:
Serie Plaza von Elledue.

Elledue Plaza series.

Série Plaza de chez Elledue.

Serie Plaza von Elledue.

Roca Georgia model.

*Mod. Georgia
de chez Roca.*

Modell Georgia
von Roca.

Roca Brocante model.

Mod. Brocante de chez Roca.

Modell Brocante von Roca.

Roca bathroom.

Salle de bain de chez Roca.

Bad von Roca.

Roca Madeira model.

Mod. Madeira de chez Roca.

Modell Madeira von Roca.

Roca Astoria model.

Mod. Astoria de chez Roca.

Modell Astoria von Roca.

Elledue Plaza model.

Série Plaza de chez Elledue.

Serie Plaza von Elledue.

Elledue Plaza model.

Série Plaza de chez Elledue.

Serie Plaza von Elledue.

Armario auxiliar de la
serie Plaza de Elledue.

*Meuble auxiliaire de la série
Plaza de chez Elledue.*

Hilfsschrank aus der
Serie Plaza von Elledue.

Elledue Plaza series vanity
table with drop-in sink.

*Lavabo coiffeuse de la série
Plaza de chez Elledue.*

Toiletten- und Waschtisch
aus der Serie Plaza
von Elledue.

Villeroy Hommage model.

Mod. Hommage de chez Villeroy.

Modell Hommage von Villeroy.

Villeroy Hommage model.

Mod. Hommage de chez Villeroy.

Modell Hommage von Villeroy.

Detail of Copat vanity.

*Détail d'un lavabo
coiffeuse de chez Copat.*

Detailansicht eines
Wasch- und Toilettentisches
von Copat.

Preceding page:
Villeroy Hommage model.

*Page suivante:
Mod. Hommage
de chez Villeroy.*

Auf der folgenden Seite:
Modell Hommage von
Villeroy.

Copat sink.

Lavabo de chez Copat.

Elledue Plaza series
compact model.

*Meuble compacte de la série
Plaza de chez Elledue.*

Kompaktmöbelstück aus
der Serie Plaza von Elledue.

Waschbecken von Copat.

Furniture / *Le mobilier*
Möbel

The twenty-first century brings modules that multiply the scale to create dressers, vanities, or storage spaces under the sink. Mirrors on sliding doors close closets or are raised sash-window style. In the classical style, some of the furniture is glimpsed through frosted glass. The aseptic character of professional installations prefers oval forms in modules of different heights with a variety of drawers and doors. Marble contrasts with tropical woods as the quality material of the vanity tops. The key idea is to select furnishings that are transportable from one residence to another thanks to the modular or freestanding concepts.

Le XXI ème siècle nous a apporté tout une série d'éléments pour créer des tiroirs, des commodes et des meubles pour la partie inférieur des lavabos. Les miroirs renferment des armoires avec des portes coulissantes ou qui s'élèvent en guillotine. Dans le style classique, certains tiroirs laissent le linge de maison à porté de la vue derrière des vitrines en cristal mat. L'asepsie des installations professionnelles nous apportent des éléments de formes ovales à différentes hauteurs avec une grande variété de tiroirs et de portes. Le marbre s'oppose aux bois tropicaux comme matériaux de qualité pour les dessus de meubles . L'idée principale maintenant c'est de choisir des meubles transportables d'un appartement à l'autre grâce à leur agencement modulaire.

Das einundzwanzigste Jahrhundert bringt Module mit sich, welche die Skala zum Schaffen von Schubläden, Komoden oder Möbel für den Platz unter dem Waschbecken multipliziert. Spiegel schlieBen Schränke durch Schiebeführungen oder lassen sich wie Guillotinen öffnen. Im klassischen Stil lassen einige Schubladen ihre Ausstattung hinter mattiertem Glas erahnen. Die Keimfreiheit der professionellen Instalationen bringt ovale Formen in Modulen mit verschiedenen Höhen und einer Flexibilität in Schubladen und Türen mit sich. Marmor kontrastiert tropische Hölzer als das Material für Qualitätsoberflächen. Die Schlüsselidee ist das Auswählen von, von einer Wohnung in die andere transportierbaren Möbeln dank dem Grundgedanken des Moduls oder des freistehenden Möbelstücks.

Previous page:
Teo-Gaia/Elledue model.

Page précédente:
Mod. Teo-Gaia
de chez Elledue.

Auf der vorherigen Seite:
Modell Teo-Gaia von Elledue.

Detail of Teo-Gaia/Elledue model.

Détail du mod. Teo-Gaia
de chez Elledue.

Detailansicht des Modells
Teo-Gaia von Elledue.

Three variations of
Teo-Gaia/Elledue model.

*Trois versions du mod. Teo-Gaia
de chez Elledue.*

Drei Abwandlungen des
Modells Teo-Gaia von Elledue.

437

Detail of Teo-Gaia/Elledue model
storage module with drawers.

*Détail d'un secrétaire du
mod. Teo-Gaia de chez Elledue.*

Detailansicht des Sekretärs des
Modells Teo-Gaia von Elledue.

Detail of the lower drawer space
in Teo-Gaia/Elledue model.

*Détail d'un tiroir du modèle
Teo-Gaia de chez Elledue.*

Detailansicht des
Schubladenmodells
Teo-Gaia von Elledue.

Teo-Gaia/Elledue
model, detail.

*Détail de mod. Teo-Gaia
de chez Elledue.*

Detailansicht
Modell Teo-Gaia
von Elledue.

Detail of Teo-Gaia/Elledue
model cabinet.

*Détail d'un meuble du modèle
Teo-Gaia de chez Elledue.*

Detailansicht des Schrankes des
Modells Teo-Gaia von Elledue.

439

Teo-Gaia/Elledue model, detail.

Détail du modèle Teo-Gaia de chez Elledue.

Detailansicht des Modells Teo-Gaia von Elledue.

Teo-Gaia/Elledue model.

Mod. Teo-Gaia de chez Elledue.

Modell Teo-Gaia von Elledue.

Three variations of
Teo-Gaia/Elledue model.

*Trois versions du mod.
Teo-Gaia de chez Elledue.*

**Drei Abwandlungen des
Modells Teo-Gaia
von Elledue.**

Two detailed views of
Teo-Gaia/Elledue model.

*Deux détails du mod.
Teo-Gaia de chez Elledue.*

Zwei Detailansichten des
Modells Teo-Gaia
von Elledue.

Teo-Gaia/Elledue model.

Mod. Teo-Gaia de chez Elledue.

Modell Teo-Gaia von Elledue.

Details of the finishes of the Elledue Plaza series.

Détails des finitions de la série Plaza de chez Elledue.

Detailansicht der Ausfertigungen aus der Serie Plaza von Elledue.

Details of the rustic finishes
of the Elledue Plaza series.

*Détails de fronts rustiques de
la série Plaza de chez Elledue.*

Detailansicht der rustikalen
Front aus der Serie Plaza
von Elledue.

Detail of the Elledue Plaza
series vanity/cabinet.

*Détail d'une coiffeuse de la
série Plaza de chez Elledue.*

Detailansicht des
Toilettentisches aus der
Serie Plaza von Elledue.

Enzo Lagno design
for Alchemy.

*Design d'Enzo Lagno
pour Alchemy.*

Entwurf von Enzo Lagno
für Alchemy.

Villeroy Hommage model
storage module.

*Meuble auxiliaire mod.
Hommage de chez Villeroy.*

Zusatzmöbel
Model Hommage von Villeroy.

Copat Zodiac series.

Série Zodiac de chez Copat.

Serie Zodiaco von Copat.

Detail of Copat
Zodiac model.

*Détail d'un meuble sous
lavabo de chez Copat.*

Detailansicht des
Möbelstücks unter dem
Waschbecken von Copat.

Detail, Copat
marble-topped vanity
auxiliary unit.

*Détail d'un tiroir avec
dessus en marbre
de chez Copat.*

Detailansicht der
Schubladenkommode mit
Marmorplatte
von Copat.

Detail of Copat Zodiac model.

Détail d'un coté du mod. Zodiaco de chez Copat.

Seitliche Detailansicht des Modells Zodiaco von Copat.

Teo-Gaia/Elledue model.

Mod. Teo-Gaia de chez Elledue.

Modell Teo-Gaia von Elledue.

Teo-Gaia/Elledue model.

Mod. Teo-Gaia de chez Elledue.

Modell Teo-Gaia von Elledue.

Two details of Teo-Gaia/Elledue model.

Deux détails du mod. Teo-Gaia de chez Elledue.

Zwei Detailansichten des Modells Teo-Gaia von Elledue.

Detail of Teo-Gaia/Elledue model.

Détail de mod. Teo-Gaia de chez Elledue.

Detailansicht des Modells Teo-Gaia von Elledue.

Detail of legs on a
Teo-Gaia/Elledue model.

*Détail des pattes d'un modèle
Teo-Gaia de chez Elledue.*

Detailansicht der FüBe eines
Modells von Teo-Gaia von Elledue.

Detail of Teo-Gaia/Elledue model.

Détail du mod. Teo-Gaia de chez Elledue.

Detailansicht des Modells Teo-Gaia von Elledue.

Detail of Teo-Gaia/Elledue model.

Détail du mod. Teo-Gaia de chez Elledue.

Detailansicht des Modells Teo-Gaia von Elledue.

Detail of Teo-Gaia/Elledue model.

Détail du mod. Teo-Gaia de chez Elledue.

Detailansicht des Modells Teo-Gaia von Elledue.

Villeroy Nagano model lamp.

Lampe mod. Nagano de chez Villeroy.

Lampe Modell Nagano von Villeroy.

Detail of a Teo-Gaia/Elledue storage module.

Détail d'un meuble auxiliaire Teo-Gaia de chez Elledue.

Detailansicht eines Zusatzmöbelstücks Teo-Gaia von Elledue.

Detail of Teo-Gaia/Elledue model.

*Détail du mod. Teo-Gaia
de chez Elledue.*

Detailansicht des
Modells Teo-Gaia von Elledue.

Preceding page:
Teo-Gaia/Elledue model.

*Page suivante:
Mod. Teo-Gaia de chez Elledue.*

Auf der folgenden Seite:
Modell Teo-Gaia von Elledue.

Detail of auxiliary
Teo-Gaia/Elledue units.

*Meubles auxiliaires
Teo-Gaia de chez Elledue.*

Zusatzmöbel
Teo-Gaia von Elledue.

Teo-Gaia/Elledue model.

Mod. Teo-Gaia de chez Elledue.

Modell Teo-Gaia von Elledue.

Laufen storage cabinet.

Meuble auxiliaire de chez Laufen.

Zusätzlicher Schrank von Laufen.

Laufen low storage unit.

*Meuble avec une porte
de chez Laufen.*

Eintüriger Schrank
von Laufen.

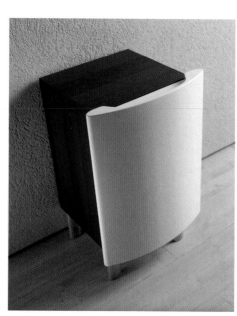

Laufen sliding mirror.

*Meuble avec miroir
coulissant de chez Laufen.*

Spiegelschiebetürschrank
von Laufen.

Laufen 3-compartment
storage module.

*Meuble auxiliaire avec 3
portes de chez Laufen.*

Zusätzlicher dreitüriger
Schrank von Laufen.

465

Sinks / *Les lavabos*
Waschgelegenheiten

Many variations are possible due to the combination of different materials: glass with steel, porcelains with tropical woods... The predictable changes add beauty. Circular drop-in sinks share the bill with woods like *jofaina*, *bacía*, or *embudo*. Rectangular models, according to their functions, reduce their depth, and are sometimes recessed, at others in glass or marble vanity tops that are extra-thin. The classic models take advantage of malleable materials to form shapes adaptable to corners. They gain depth while disappearing into the marble top of the vanity. Some eccentric models hark back to liberty artisanship, working the composition of the original materials to create works of art.

Il existe beaucoup de variations grâce au croisement de différents matériaux: verre et acier, porcelaine et bois tropicaux, qui changent de forme de manière imprévisible pour les rendre encore plus baux. Les lave-mains circulaires se déguisent en réceptacle, récipient ou en cuve pendant que les rectangulaires réduisent la profondeur de leur bac selon leur fonctionnalité, parfois encastrés et d'autres en dessous d'une superficie en verre ou en marbre extra plat. Les modèles classiques profitent de la malléabilité des matériaux pour adopter des formes arrondies et augmenter leur profondeur toute fois qu'ils tendent à disparaître sous un support en marbre. Certains modèles excentriques rappellent l'artisanat des imprimés Liberty qui conjuguent des matériaux originaux pour créer de véritables œuvres d'art.

Man erreicht groBe Variationen durch die Kreuzung von Materialien: Glas mit Stahl, Porzelan mit tropischen Hölzern, welches die sichtbaren Formen verschönern. Kreisförmige Waschbecken verkleiden sich als Trichter oder Behälter. Während rechteckige die Vertiefung je nach ihrer Funktionalität reduzieren, manchmal als eingebaute Waschbecken, manchmal auf Glasplatten oder extraflachen Marmorplatten. Die klassischen Modelle nützen die Biegsamkeit des Materials, um nierenförmig zu erscheinen und an Tiefe in dem MaBe in dem sie in der Marmorplatte verschwinden zu gewinnen. Manche extravaganten Modelle verweisen auf das Libertykunsthandwerk in dem sie mit der Verbindung von originellen Materialien arbeiten um so Kunstwerke zu schaffen.

Previous page:
P. Starck's Mini designs
for Duravit.

Page précédente:
Design Mini de P. Starck
pour Duravit.

Auf der vorherigen Seite:
Entwurf Mini von P.
Starck für Duravit.

Altro Miniaqua model.

Mod. Miniaqua de chez Altro.

Modell Miniaqua von Altro.

Teo-Gaia/Elledue
porcelain sink.

Lavabo en porcelaine
mod. Teo-gaia
de chez Elledue.

Porzelanwaschbecken
Teo-Gaia von Elledue.

Teo-Gaia/Elledue
drop-in sink.

Lavabo encastré
mod. Teo-Gaia
de chez Elledue.

Eingebautes
Waschbecken
Teo-Gaia von Elledue.

Teo-Gaia/Elledue
rectangular sink with
beveled edges.

Lavabo rectangulaire
avec rebords courbés
mod. Teo-Gaia
de chez Elledue.

Rechteckiges
Waschbecken mit
gerundeten Rändern
Teo-Gaia von Elledue.

| Two Teo-Gaia/ Elledue freestanding models. | Deux modèles indépendants mod. Teo-Gaia de chez Elledue. | Zwei freistehende Modelle Teo-Gaia von Elledue. | Teo-Gaia/Elledue model. | Mod. Teo-Gaia de chez Elledue. | Modell Teo-Gaia von Elledue. |

Teo-Gaia/Elledue model.

Mod. Teo-Gaia de chez Elledue.

Modell Teo-Gaia von Elledue.

Details of freestanding Teo-Gaia/Elledue sink.

Détailles d'un lavabo indépendant mod. Teo-Gaia de chez Elledue.

Detailansicht des freistehenden Waschbeckens Teo-Gaia von Elledue.

Details of freestanding
Teo-Gaia/Elledue sink.

Détailles d'un lavabo
indépendant mod. Teo-Gaia
de chez Elledue.

Detailansicht des freistehenden
Waschbeckens Teo-Gaia
von Elledue.

Teo-Gaia/Elledue model Low.

Mod. Low
Teo-Gaia de chez Elledue.

Modell Low von
Teo-Gaia von Elledue.

471

A Teo-Gaia/Elledue
wall-mount model.

Modèle adossé au mur
Teo-Gaia de chez Elledue.

An die Wand angebautes Modell
von Teo-Gaia von Elledue.

Altro Low model.

*Mod. Low encastré
de chez Altro.*

Eingebautes Modell
Low von Altro.

Narcissus high
freestanding sink.

Modèle indépendant
en hauteur
de chez Narcissus.

Hohes freistehendes
Modell von Narcissus.

Altro Low model
drop-in sink.

Modèle Low encastré
de chez Altro.

Eingebautes Modell
Low von Altro.

Alchemy Lava Mod. with erosion edge.

Mod. Lava avec rebord rongé de chez Alchemy.

Modell Lava Randabwaschung von Alchemy.

Alchemy Fish Mod.
with erosion edge.

Mod. Fish avec rebord rongé
de chez Alchemy.

Modell Fish Randabwaschung
von Alchemy.

Alchemy Misto Mod.

Mod. Misto de chez Alchemy.

Modell Misto von Alchemy.

Alchemy Coral Mod.
on bronze tripod stand.

Mod. Coral sur piédestal
de bronze de chez Alchemy.

Modell Coral auf
Bronzesockel von Alchemy.

474

Alchemy Fish Mod.

Mod. Fish de chez Alchemy.

Modell Fish von Alchemy.

Alchemy Fósil Mod.
with polished edge.

Mod. Fosil avec rebord
poli de chez Alchemy.

Modell Fósil mit
geglättetem Rand
von Alchemy.

Alchemy Ether Mod.
with erosion edge.

Mod. Ether avec rebord
rongé de chez Alchemy.

Modell Ether mit
Erosionsrand von
Alchemy.

Alchemy model with
polished edge.

*Mod. avec rebord poli
de chez Alchemy.*

Modell mit geglättetem
Rand von Alchemy.

Alchemy Coral Mod.
with erosion edge.

Mod. Coral avec rebord
rongé de chez Alchemy.

Modell Coral mit
Erosionsrand von
Alchemy.

Alchemy Fish Mod. on stand
with sculpted legs.

Mod. Fish sur un dessus avec
pattes sculptées
de chez Alchemy.

**Modell Fish auf Platte mit
gerundeten FüBen
von Alchemy.**

Alchemy Fish Mod. with
polished edge.

Mod. Fish avec rebord poli
de chez Alchemy.

**Modell Fish mit geglättetem
Rand von Alchemy.**

Alchemy Fishwater Mod.
with erosion edge.

Mod. Fish avec rebord poli
de chez Alchemy.

**Modell Fish mit geglättetem
Rand von Alchemy.**

Alchemy Coral Mod.
with erosion edge.

Mod. Coral rongé
de chez Alchemy.

**Modell Coral mit
Erosionsvand
von Alchemy.**

Alchemy Fish Mod.
with polished edge.

Mod. Fish avec rebord poli
de chez Alchemy.

**Modell Fish mit geglättetem
Rand von Alchemy.**

Alchemy Ether Mod.
with erosion edge.

Mod. Ether avec rebord
rongé de chez Alchemy.

**Modell Ether mit
Erosionsrand von Alchemy.**

Alchemy Glacier Mod.
with semi-base.

Mod. Glacier avec demi
piédestal de chez Alchemy.

Modell Glacier mit
Halbsockel von Alchemy.

Alchemy Gold Mod.
with bronze tripod stand.

Mod. Gold avec piédestal
de bronze de chez Alchemy.

**Modell Gold mit
Bronzesockel von Alchemy.**

Alchemy Glacier Glass Mod.

Mod. Glacier Glass de chez Alchemy.

Modell Glacier Glass von Alchemy.

478

Alchemy Glacier Mod.
with polished edge.

Mod. Glacier avec rebord
poli de chez Alchemy.

Modell Glacier mit
geglättetem Rand
von Alchemy.

Mod. Alchemy Coral Ciénaga Mod. with erosion edge.

Mod. Coral Cienaga avec rebord rongé de chez Alchemy.

Modell Coral ciénaga mit Erosionsrand von Alchemy.

Alchemy Ether Mod. with polished edge on bronze tripod stand.

Mod. Ether avec rebords rongé et piédestal en bronze de chez Alchemy.

Modell Ether mit geglättenem Rand und Bronzesockel von Alchemy.

479

Tulli Curva Mod.

Mod. Curva de chez Tulli.

Modell Curva von Tulli.

Tulli Cubo Mod.

Mod. Cubo de chez Tulli.

Modell Cubo von Tulli.

Tulli Cubo Mod.

Mod. Cubo de chez Tulli.

Modell Cubo von Tulli.

Tulli Curva Mod.

Mod. Curva de chez Tulli.

Modell Curva von Tulli.

481

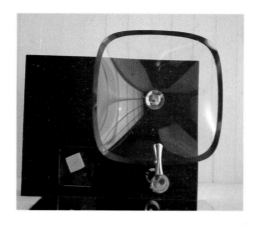

Tulli Dadi Mod.

Mod. Dadi de chez Tulli.

Modell Dadi von Tulli.

Altro Gotta Mod.

Mod. Gotta de chez Altro.

Modell Gotta von Altro.

Tulli Dadi Mod.

Mod. Dadi de chez Tulli.

Modell Dadi von Tulli.

Laufen Mod.

Différents modèles de chez Laufen.

Modell von Laufen.

Tulli Tesi Mod.

Mod. Tesi de chez Tulli.

Modell Tesi von Tulli.

Tulli Dadi Mod.

Mod. Dadi de chez Tulli.

Modell Dadi von Tulli.

Tulli Dadi Mod.

Mod. Dadi de chez Tulli.

Modell Dadi von Tulli.

Tulli Dadi Mod.

Mod. Dadi de chez Tulli.

Modell Dadi von Tulli.

Tulli Tesi Mod.

Mod. Tesi de chez Tulli.

Modell Tesi von Tulli.

Elledue Plaza series fitted sink.

Lavabo encastré arrondi
série Plaza de chez Elledue.

Eingebautes Waschbecken
in Nierenform aus der
Serie Plaza von Elledue.

Duravit semi-stand sink.

Lavabo avec demi piédestal
de chez Duravit.

Waschbecken mit Halbsockel
von Duravit.

Duravit sink and
slide-under vanity.

Lavabo sur meuble
de chez Duravit.

Waschbecken auf
Möbel von Duravit.

Duravit sink.

Lavabo avec demi piédestal
de chez Duravit.

Waschbecken mit Sockel
von Duravit.

Duravit semi-stand sink.

Lavabo avec demi
piédestal de chez
Duravit.

Waschbecken mit
Halbsockel
von Duravit.

Villeroy Soho N.Y. Mod.

Mod. Soho N.Y. de chez Villeroy.

Modell Soho. N. Y. von Villeroy.

A Starck design
for Duravit.

Un design de Starck
pour Duravit.

**Ein Entwurf von Starck
für Duravit.**

Altro Tube Mod.

Mod. Tube de chez Altro.

Modell Tube von Altro.

Duravit Vero Mod.

Mod. Vero de chez Duravit.

Mod. Vero von Duravit.

Altro Tube In Mod.

Mod. Tube In de chez Altro.

Modell Tube In von Altro.

Tulli Ondula Mod.

Mod. Ondula de chez Tulli.

Modell Ondula von Tulli.

Magma Mod.

Différents modèles
de chez Magma.

Modelle von Magma.

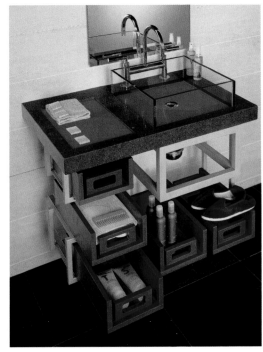

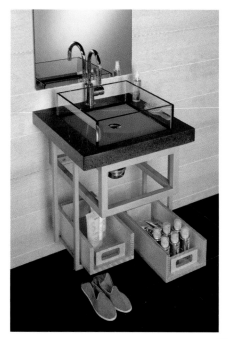

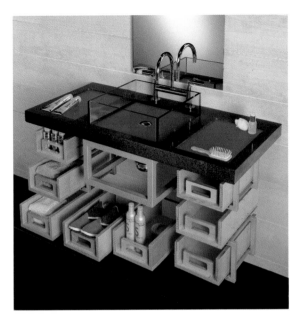

Magma Mod.

Différents modèles
de chez Magma.

Modelle von Magma.

495

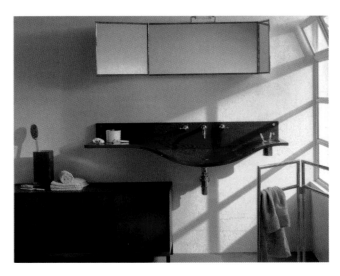

El Gabbiano sink.

Lavabo El Gabbiano.

Waschbecken El Gabbiano.

Flat sink.

Lavabo Flat.

Waschbecken Flat.

Optima sink.

Lavabo Optima.

Waschbecken Optima.

Duravit sink and stand.

Lavabo et meuble de chez Duravit.

Waschcbecken und Möbelstück
von Duravit.

Menhir sink.

Lavabo Menhir.

Waschbecken Menhir.

Morgans sink.

Lavabo Morgans.

Waschbecken Morgans.

Toilets / *Les sanitaires*
Toiletten

Porcelain rules in all models, whether base or wall-mount. One-piece models are valued for their simple bowls, which facilitate cleaning because they avoid nonfunctional groove patterns. The design includes the seats, with a preference for cool colors. The designs by Starck play with the notion of waste containers. Tanks include high, narrow models to increase flush pressure. Water-saving devices include a double button for half-flush or complete flush.

La porcelaine est devenue la reine des surfaces actuelles. On apprécie son concept de pièce unique et on étudie de près les bases qui facilitent son nettoyage en évitant des reliefs peu fonctionnels. Le design arrive jusqu'aux couvercles de waters, avec un goût remarqué pour les couleurs pâles, sans stridences. Les créations de Starck conjuguent la notion de conteneur de déchets. Il existe des modèles de réservoirs en hauteur et plus étroits qui améliorent la pression de l'eau. L'inclusion d'un double bouton permet de vider la moitié ou la totalité de la charge pour permettre d'économiser de l'eau.

Porzelan ist die Königin aller Modelle, ob am Boden oder Aufgehängtes. Man legt Wert auf das Konzept des Einzelstückes, mit Beachtung der Basis, um die Reinigung zu erleichtern und bei gleichzeitiger Vermeidung von nicht funktionalen Reliefs. Das Design hat bis zum Deckel eine Vorliebe für weiche Farben, ohne Schrillheit. Die Entwürfe von Starck spielen mit einem Hauch von Abfallbehältern. Die Spülkästen betreffend findet man hohe, schlanke Modelle, welche den Druck des Wasserstrahls verbessern. Das Wassersparen wird durch die Einführung des doppelten Druckknopfes erleichtert, welcher entweder nur die Hälfte oder den kompletten Inhalt des Spülkastens entleert.

Previous page:
Duravit toilet and bidet set.

Page précédente:
Ensemble cuvette de waters
et bidet de chez Duravit.

Auf der vorherigen Seite:
Ensemble aus Wasserklosett
und Bidet von Duravit.

Villeroy Hommage Mod.

Mod. Hommage de chez Villeroy.

Modell Hommage von Villeroy.

Roca Veranda Mod.

Mod. Veranda de chez Roca.

Modell Veranda von Roca.

Villeroy et Bosch Century
Garden Mod.

*Mod. Century Garden de
chez Villeroy et Bosch.*

Modell Century Garden
von Villeroy und Bosch.

Villeroy et Bosch Century
Titanic Mod.

*Mod. Century Titanic de
chez Villeroy et Bosch.*

Modell Century Titanic
von Villeroy und Bosch.

Duravit Caro Mod.

Mod. Caro de chez Duravit.

Modell Caro von Duravit.

Delafon Trocadero bidet.

Bidet Trocadero de chez Jacob Delafon.

Bidet Trocadero von Delafon.

Jacob Delafon Odéon bidet.

Bidet Odéon de chez Jacob Delafon.

Bidet Odeon von Jacob Delafon.

Delafon New Haven bidet.

Bidet New Haven de chez Jacob Delafon.

Bidet New Haven von Delafon.

Delafon portrait bidet.

Mod. Portait de chez Jacob Delafon.

Modell Portrait von Delafon.

Delafon Fleur Mod.

Mod. Fleur de chez Jacob Delafon.

Modell Fleur von Delafon.

Jacob Delafon Antores Mod.

Mod. Antores de chez Jacob Delafon.

Modell Antores von Delafon.

Roca retro style bidet.

Bidet style rétro de chez Roca.

Bidet im alten Stil, von Roca.

504

Villeroy et Bosch Century Titanic toilet.

Cuvette de waters Century Titanic de chez Villeroy et Bosch.

Wasserklosett Century Titanic von Villeroy et Bosch.

Delafon Astros Mod.

Mod. Astros de chez Jacob Delafon.

Modell Astros von Delafon.

Roca Veranda bidet.

Bidet Veranda chez Roca.

Bidet Veranda von Roca.

Delafon Altair Mod.

Mod. Altair de chez Jacob Delafon.

Modell Altair von Delafon.

Roca Dama Mod.

Mod. Dama de chez Roca.

Modell Dama von Roca.

Roca Victoria Mod.

Victoria de chez Roca.

Modell Victoria von Roca.

Roca Meridian Mod.

Mod. Meridan de chez Roca.

Modell Meridian von Roca.

Roca Veranda Mod.

Mod. Veranda de chez Roca.

Modell Veranda von Roca.

Roca Verónica Mod.

Mod Veronica de chez Roca.

Modell Verónica von Roca.

Roca Georgia Mod.

Mod. Georgia de chez Roca.

Modell Georgia von Roca.

Roca Sydney Mod.

Mod. Sydney de chez Roca.

Modell Sydney von Roca.

Roca Meridian Mod.

Mod. Meridian de chez Roca.

Modell Meridian von Roca.

Roca Urinett Mod.

Mod. Urinett de chez Roca.

Modell Urinett von Roca.

Roca Verónica Mod.

Mod. Veronica de chez Roca.

Modell Verónica von Roca.

Roca Veranda Mod.

Mod. Veranda de chez Roca.

Modell Veranda von Roca.

Aro reductor adaptável
Roca Pony Mod.

*Anneau réducteur mod. Pony
de chez Roca.*

Angepasster Verkleinerungsring
Modell Pony, von Roca.

Roca Multifunción Mod.

Mod. Multifonction de chez Roca.

Modell Multifunción von Roca.

Roca Multiclin Mod.

Siège couvercle Multiclin de chez Roca.

Sitz und Deckel Multiclin, von Roca.

wall-suspension bidet and toilet set.

Ensemble bidet et cuvette de waters suspendus.

Spannendes Ensemble aus Bidet und Toilette.

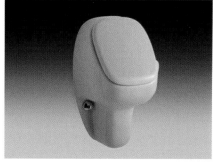

Roca Urinett Mod.

Mod. Urinett de chez Roca.

Modell Urinett von Roca.

Duravit wall-mount set.

Ensemble suspendu de chez Duravit.

Hängendes Ensemble von Duravit.

Duravit McDry Mod.

Mod. McDry de chez Duravit.

Modell McDry von Duravit.

Villeroy Editionals Mod.

Mod. Editionals de chez Villeroy.

Modell Editionals von Villeroy.

Laconda wall-mount
toilet.

*Sanitaires suspendu
de chez Laconda.*

Aufgehängte Toiletten
von Laconda.

Laufen Mod.

Model de chez Laufen.

Modell von Laufen.

Laufen Mod. with slim tank.

*Mod. avec réservoir étroit
de chez Laufen.*

**Modell mit schlankem
Spülkasten von Laufen.**

Laufen Mod. toilet with
concealed tank.

*Cuvette de waters avec
réservoir encastré
de chez Laufen.*

Wasserklosett mit
eingebautem Spülkasten
von Laufen.

Laufen freestanding model.

Bidet indépendant de chez Laufen.

Freistehendes Bidet von Laufen.

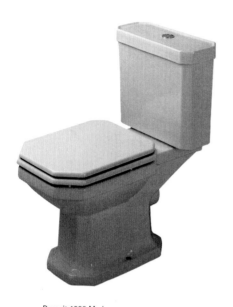

Duravit 1939 Mod.

Mod. 1939 de chez Duravit.

Modell 1939 von Duravit.

Duravit Caro Mod.

Mod. Caro de chez Duravit.

Modell Caro von Duravit.

Duravit Architect Mod.

Mod. Architect de chez Duravit.

Modell Architect von Duravit.

Duravit Darling Mod.

Mod. Darling de chez Duravit.

Modell Darling von Duravit.

Jacob Delafon Altair toilet.

Mod. Altair de chez Jacob Delafon.

Modell Altair von Delafon.

Duravit Dell'Asco Mod.

Mod. Dell'Arco de chez Duravit.

Modell Dell'Arco von Duravit.

Duravit wall-suspension
Darling Mod.

*Mod. Darling suspendu
de chez Duravit.*

Modell Darling aufgehängt
von Duravit.

Duravit Caro Mod.

Mod. Caro de chez Duravit.

Modell Caro von Duravit.

Starck urinal designed for Duravit.

Urinoir de Satrck pour Duravit.

Urinal von Starck für Duravit.

Starck toilet for Duravit.

Cuvette de waters de Starck pour Duravit.

Wasserklosett von Starck für Duravit.

Starck wall-suspension
toilet for Duravit.

*Cuvette de waters suspendue
de Starck pour Duravit.*

Hängendes Wasserklosett
von Starck für Duravit.

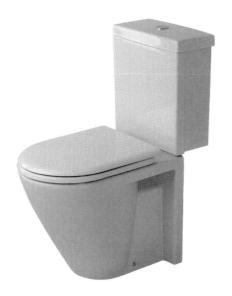

Starck toilet for Duravit.

Mod. de Starck pour Duravit.

Modell von Starck für Duravit.

Duravit Duravital Mod.

Mod. Duravital de chez Duravit.

Modell Duravital von Duravit.

Starck toilet for Duravit.

Cuvette de waters de Starck pour Duravit.

Wasserklosett von Starck für Duravit.

Accessories / *Les accessoires*
Zubehör

___

Accessory designs for the bathroom serve as ornamentation for each object. The materials-wood, porcelain, steel, or plastic-are those usually found in this room. They are used because they are water-resistant. Functionalism is not incompatible with imagination: we find that each element comes off the drawing board with an eye to novelty and discovery, minimalist sculpture of a great degree of formal abstraction.

L'élégance est le point commun de chacun des accessoires conçus pour les salles de bain. Les matériaux comme le bois, la porcelaine, l'acier ou le plastique, très côtés dans ce domaine, sont réalisés avec un traitement contre l'humidité. La fonctionnalité ne va pas nécessairement à l'encontre de l'imagination . C'est pour cela que chaque élément a été crée comme un objet très spéciale, presque comme une sculpture minimaliste qui concentre jusqu' à l'abstraction l' essence de chaque accessoire.

Das Design der Zubehörteile für das Badezimmer gibt jedem Objekt seine Eleganz. Die Materialien, Holz, Porzelan, Stahl oder Plastik, sind die üblichen für diese Stücke, die für das Standhalten in Feuchtigkeit gedacht sind. Die Funktionalität wiederspricht nicht der Fantasie und so finden wir, daB jedes Objekt als spezielles Werk gedacht scheint, eine minimalistische Skulptur bis hin zum Konzentrat des Erreichens von maximaler Abstraktheit, ergibt die Essenz eines jeden Objekts

Preceding page:
Siria set of bathroom
accessories in steel and plastic.

Page précédente:
Ensemble d'accessoires en acier
et plastique de chez Siria.

Auf der vorherigen Seite:
Ensemble von Zubehörteilen
in Stahl und Plastik von Siria.

Detail, Tulli towel bar.

Détail d'un porte-serviette
métallique de chez Tulli.

Detailansicht eines metallenen
Handtuchhalters von Tulli.

Teo-Gaia/Elledue Mod.
toilet tissue holder.

Porte-rouleau de papier mod.
Teo-Gaia de chez Elledue.

Toilettenpapierhalter Modell
Teo-Gaia von Elledue.

Teo-Gaia/Elledue Mod. towel hooks.

Crochets à vêtements mod. Teo-Gia de chez Elledue.

Kleiderhaken Modell Teo-Gaia von Elledue.

Teo-Gaia/Elledue Mod. brush.

Balayette mod. Teo-Gaia de chez Elledue.

Toilettenbürste Modell Teo-Gaia von Elledue.

Teo-Gaia/Elledue Mod. towel hooks.

Porte-serviette mod. Teo-Gaia de chez Elledue.

Handtuchhalter Modell Teo-Gaia von Elledue.

Teo-Gaia/Elledue Mod. toothbrush holder.

Support de verre mod. Teo-Gaia de chez Elledue.

Glashalter Modell Teo-Gaia von Elledue.

Teo-Gaia/Elledue Mod. soap dish.

Porte-savon mod. Teo-Gaia de chez Elledue.

Seifenschale Modell Teo-Gaia von Elledue.

Teo-Gaia/Elledue Mod. towel bar.

Porte-serviette mod. Teo-Gaia de chez Elledue.

Handtuchhalter Modell Teo-Gaia von Elledue.

Teo-Gaia/Elledue Mod. toothbrush holder.

Support de verre mod. Teo-Gaia de chez Elledue.

Glashalter Modell Teo-Gaia von Elledue.

Teo-Gaia/Elledue Mod.
soap dish.

*Porte-savon mod. Teo-Gaia
de chez Elledue.*

Seifenschale Modell
von Teo-Gaia/Elledue.

Teo-Gaia/Elledue Mod. toilet tissue holder.

*Porte-rouleau de papier mod. Teo-Gaia
de chez Elledue.*

Toilettenpapierhalter Modell Teo-Gaia
von Elledue.

Teo-Gaia/Elledue Mod.
towel hooks.

*Crochets à vêtement mod.
Teo-Gaia de chez Elledue.*

Kleiderhaken Modell Teo-Gaia
von Elledue.

Teo-Gaia/Elledue Mod. brush.

*Balayette mod. Teo-Gaia
de chez Elledue.*

Toilettenbürste Modell
Teo-Gaia von Elledue.

523

Altro Onix Mod. toilet accessory set.

Ensemble mod. Onix de chez Altro.

Ensemble Modell Onix von Altro.

Marat towel bar and shelf set.

Jeux de porte-serviettes et étagères de chez Marat.

Serie von Handtuchhaltern und Regalen von Marat.

Altro Onix Mod. mirror.

Miroir mod. Onix de chez Altro.

Spiegel Modell Onix von Altro.

Marat toilet accessory set.

Ensemble d'accessoires de chez Marat.

Ensemble von Zubehörteilen von Marat.

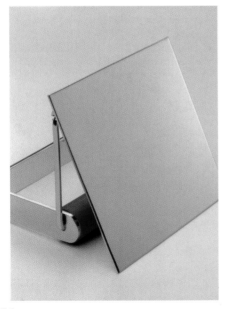

Faucets / *Le Robineterie*
Armaturen

The most advanced technology has introduced thermostatic and electronic models to allow users to control the temperature of the water at their convenience. This facilitates both energy conservation and time. Insulating materials for faucet finishes, chromed and plastic, guarantee optimal quality and safety in the use of these elements. Ergonomic design blends aesthetics with functionalism and also conceals the smart technology inside. This presentation keeps the traditional advances: twist action in the classic dual control; button controls for newer, more stylized models; and half-turn levers for single control faucets.

La technologie la plus avancée présente des modèles thermostatiques et électroniques pour contrôler la température de l'eau selon la convenance, autant par économie d'énergie et de temps. Pour les revêtements, chromés ou plastiques, les matériaux isolants garantissent une qualité et une sécurité maximums lors de l'utilisation de ces éléments. Le design ergonomique conjuguent l'esthétique avec la fonctionnalité et cache son haut degré d'intelligence dans son intérieur. Du coté de la présentation , le succès réside dans les modèles consolidés : le robinet à manette pour les modèles classiques qui recherchent un air nostalgique, le robinet à pression pour les plus stylisés et la manette d'un demi tour pour les mélangeurs monoblocs.

Die neueste Technologie bietet uns thermostatische und elektrische Modelle, welche die Wassertemparatur zweckmässig kontrollieren, sowohl mit Blick auf das Energiesparen als auch im Sinne des Zeitaufwands. Isolierende Materialien für die Verkleidung, seien es nun verchromte oder aus Plastik, garantieren maximale Qualität und Sicherheit im Umgang mit diesen Bestandteilen. Ein ergonomisches Design kombiniert Ästhetik mit Funktionalität und versteckt dabei seine intelligente Innenstruktur. Die Präsentation bleibt bei den gefestigten Erfolgen: Der Drehgriff für die klassischen Modelle, die einen Hauch Nostalgie suchen, der Druckknopf für die Stilvollsten und der zurückkehrende zentrierte Hebel für Mischgeräte mit nur einem Griff.

Previous page:
Dornbracht Tara Mod.

Pag. précédente:
Mod. Tara de chez
Dornbracht.

Auf der vorherigen Seite:
Modell Tara
von Dornbracht.

Grohe Eurostyle single
control faucet.

Robinet monobloc Eurostyle
de chez Grohe.

Einfacher Griff
Eurostyle von Grohe.

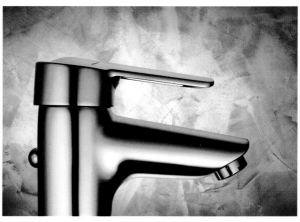

Dornbracht Tara Mod.
lever control faucet

*Robinet à manette mod. Tara
de chez Dornbracht.*

Hebelgriff Modell Tara
von Dornbracht.

Dorn Emote button control faucet.

*Robinet mural avec bouton à pression
Emote de chez Dorn.*

Wandhahn mit Druckknopf
Emote von Dorn.

Roca Verona Mod.
hand-held shower

*Douche téléphone
mod. Verona de chez Roca.*

Telefondusche
Modell Verona von Roca.

Roca shower arm.

Tube mural de chez Roca.

Wandröhre von Roca.

Roca Verona Mod.
hand-held shower.

*Douche téléphone
mod. Verona de chez Roca.*

Telefondusche
Modell Verona von Roca.

Roca Florentina Mod.
hand-held shower.

*Douche téléphone
mod. Florentina de chez Roca.*

Telefondusche
Modell Florentina von Roca.

Roca Verona Mod.
dual control faucet.

*Mélangeur mod. Verona
de chez Roca.*

Mischwasserhaln
Modell Verona von Roca.

Roca Florentina Mod.
dual control faucet.

*Mélangeur
mod. Florentina
de chez Roca.*

Mischwasserhaln
Modell Florentina
von Roca.

Roca Florentina Mod.
dual control faucet.

*Mélangeur
mod. Florentina
de chez Roca.*

Mischwasserhaln
Modell Florentina
von Roca.

Roca Florentina Mod.
dual control faucet.

*Mélangeur
mod. Florentina de chez Roca.*

Mischwasserhaln
Modell Florentina von Roca.

Roca Medio Mod. single
control faucet.

*Mélangeur mod. Medio
de chez Roca.*

Mischwasserhaln Modell
Medio von Roca.

Roca Verona Mod.
dual control faucet.

*Mélangeur mod. Verona
de chez Roca.*

Mischwasserhaln Modell
Verona von Roca.

Roca Brava
Mod. dual control faucet.

*Mélangeur mod. Brava
de chez Roca.*

Mischwasserhaln Modell
Brava von Roca.

Roca Florentina Mod.
dual control faucet.

*Mélangeur mod. Florentina
de chez Roca.*

Mischwasserhaln Modell
Florentina von Roca.

Roca Amura Mod. dual control faucet.

Mélangeur mod. Amura de chez Roca.

Mischbatterie Modell Amura von Roca.

Roca Lógica Mod.
single control faucet.
Mélangeur mod.
Logica de chez Roca.
Mischbatterie
Modell Lógica
von Roca.

Roca a M2 Mod.
single control faucet.
Mélangeur mod.
Monomando M2
de chez Roca
Mischbatterie Modell
Monomando M2
von Roca.

Roca Monojet Mod.
single control faucet.

Mélangeur mod. Monojet
de chez Roca.

Mischbatterie
Modell Monojet von Roca.

Roca Monodín Mod.
single control faucet.
Mélangeur mod.
Monodin de chez
Roca.
Mischbatterie
Modell Monodín
von Roca.

Roca Victoria Mod.
single control faucet.

Mélangeur mod. Victoria
Plus de chez Roca.

Mischbatterie
Modell Victoria Plus von Roca.

Roca Victoria Mod.
single control faucet.
Mélangeur
mod. Victoria
de chez Roca.
Mischbatterie
Modell Victoria
von Roca.

533

Roca Panamá Mod. swivel faucet.

Robinet giratoire mod. Panama de chez Roca.

Drehgriff Modell Panamá von Roca.

Roca Amura Mod. electronic control faucet.

Mélangeur électronique mod. Amura de chez Roca.

Elektrische Mischbatterie Modell Amura von Roca.

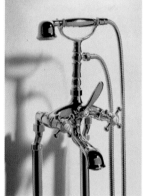

Roca Verona Mod. dual control tub
faucet and hand-held shower.

*Robinetterie de bain et douche
mod. Verona de chez Roca.*

Badewannenhahn und Dusche
Modell Verona von Roca.

Roca Modena Mod.
single control faucet.

*Monobloc mod. Modena
de chez Roca.*

Einfacher Griff
Modell Modena von Roca.

Roca Atai Mod.
lever control faucet.

*Robinet avec manette
mod. Atai de chez Roca.*

Hebelgriff
Modell Atai von Roca.

Roca Lógica Mod. single control
swivel faucet.

*Mélangeur avec tube giratoire
mod. Logica de chez Roca.*

Mischabatterie mit drehbarer
Röhre Modell Lógica von Roca.

Roca Panamá Mod.
double control swivel faucet.

*Mélangeur avec tube giratoire
mod. Panama de chez Roca.*

Mischwasserhahn mit drehbarer
Röhre Modell Panamá von Roca.

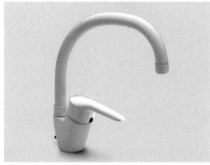

Roca Lógica Mod.
single control swivel faucet

*Monobloc avec tube giratoire
mod. Logica de chez Roca.*

Einfacher Griff mit drehbarem Rohr
Modell Lógica von Roca.

Roca Lógica Mod.
single control swivel faucet

*Monobloc avec tube giratoire
mod. Logica de chez Roca.*

Einfacher Griff mit drehbarem Rohr
Modell Lógica von Roca.

535

Villeroy Square
Mod. double control faucet.

*Mélangeur mod. Square
de chez Villeroy.*

Mischwasserhahn Modell
Square von Villeroy.

Villeroy Square Mod.
double control basin-ledge faucet.

*Robinetterie sur console
mod. Square de chez Villeroy.*

Kragsteinarmaturen
Modell Square von Villeroy.

Villeroy Square Mod.
double control basin-ledge faucet.

*Robinetterie sur console
mod. Square de chez Villeroy.*

Kragsteinarmaturen
Modell Square von Villeroy.

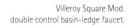

536

Villeroy Circle Mod.
single control faucet.

Robinetterie su console mod.
Circle de chez Villeroy.

Kragsteinarmaturen
Modell Circle von Villeroy.

Villeroy Circle Mod.
single control faucet.

Monobloc mod. Circle
de chez Villeroy.

Einfacher Griff
Modell Circle von Villeroy.

Villeroy Circle Mod.
single control faucet.

Monobloc mod. Circle
de chez Villeroy.

Einfacher Griff
Modell Circle von Villeroy.

Villeroy Circle 5 Mod. double
control basin-ledge faucet.

Robinetterie sur console
mod. Circle de chez Villeroy.

Kragsteinarmaturen
Modell Circle von Villeroy.

Dornbracht Meta Mod.
single control faucet.

*Monobloc mod. Meta
de chez Dornbracht.*

**Einfacher Griff
Modell Meta
von Dornbracht.**

Grohe Tectron Mod. sink faucet
and shower head.

*Robinetterie de lavabo et douche
mod. Tectron de chez Grohe.*

**Armaturen für Dusche und WC
Modell Tectron von Grohe.**

Grohe Eurosmart Mod.
single control faucet.

*Monobloc mod. Eurosmart
de chez Grohe.*

Einfacher Griff
Modell Eurosmart von Grohe.

Grohe Ectos Mod.
single control glass lever faucet.

*Monobloc avec manette en verre
mod. Ectos de chez Grohe.*

Einfacher Griff mit Glashebel
Modell Ectos von Grohe.

Bathtubs / *Les baignoires*
Badewannen

Modern bathtubs are so playful that the question of hygiene seems to take second place. The equivalent would be a family spa, with the body cult a derivative of the science of health. Bathtubs are sunken, fitted, attached to the wall, or freestanding. Mini-pools are just one more step toward the dream, along with hydromassage or musical therapy in some styles. The materials (porcelain, cast iron, or acrylics) are molded to adopt any shape, no matter how capricious. The role of the finishes, apart from the aesthetic, is to guarantee the users' safety.

Les baignoires modernes ont à présent un côté si ludique que l'hygiène proprement dite parait reléguée au deuxième rang. L'équivalant serait représenté par le balnéaire familial et le culte au corps comme dérivé de la science qui s'occupe de la santé. Il existe des baignoires encastrées, adossées au mur ou indépendantes. Les mini piscines nous invitent à rêver tout comme les prouesses de l'hydro massage ou de la musicothérapie. Les matériaux (porcelaine, fonte ou acryliques) sont moulés pour adopter n'importe qu'elle forme si capricieuse soit elle. Les finitions se chargent, de leur coté, d'assurer la sécurité de l'usager.

Die modernen Badewannen präsentieren so eindeutig eine spielerische Absicht, daB die Frage der Hygiene scheinbar in den Hintergrund verwiesen wird. Das Equivalent wäre das Familienheilbad oder der Körperkult als Abwandlung der Heilwissenschaft. Die Badewannen präsentieren sich eingebaut, an Wände angebaut oder freistehend. Minischwimmbäder sind der nächste Schritt zum Traum, zusammen mit den Leistungen der Druckstrahlmassage oder der in einigen Lösungen angebotenen Musiktherapie. Die Materialien (Porzelan, gegossenes Eisen oder Acryl) nehmen jegliche Form an, so ausgefallen sie auch sein mag. Die Ausführungen teilen sich die Mission der Sicherheitsgarantie für den Benutzer.

Previous page:
Laufen Mod.

Page précédente:
Modèle de chez Laufen.

Auf der vorherigen Seite:
Modell von Laufen.

Hoesch oval bathtub.

Baignoire ovale de chez Hoesch.

Ovale Badewanne von Hoesch.

Curas Veranda Mod. with screen.

Mod. Veranda avec paravent de chez Curas.

Modell Veranda mit Trennwand von Curas.

Roca Aruba Mod.

Mod. Aruba de chez Roca.

Modell Aruba von Roca.

Roca Varadero Mod.

Mod. Varadero de chez Roca.

Modell Varadero von Roca.

Roca Waikiki Mod.

Mod. Waikiki de chez Roca.

Modell Waikiki von Roca.

Roca Bali Mod.

Mod. Bali de chez Roca.

Modell Bali von Roca.

Roca Waitara Mod.

Mod. Waitara en angle droit de chez Roca.

Modell Waitara mit Eckevechts, von Roca.

Roca Waitara Mod.

Mod. Waitara en angle gauche de chez Roca.

Modell Waitara mit Ecke links, von Roca.

Roca Hawai Mod.

Mod. Hawai avec deux dossiers de chez Roca.

Modell Hawai mit zwei Lehnen von Roca.

Roca Fragata Mod.

Mod. Fragata de chez Roca.

Modell Fragata von Roca.

Roca Qualia Mod.

Mod. Qualia de chez Roca.

Modell Qualia von Roca.

Roca Miami Mod.

Mod. Miami de chez Roca.

Modell Miami von Roca.

Roca Catamaran Mod.

Mod. Catamaran de chez Roca.

Modell Catamarán von Roca.

Roca Levante Mod.

Mod. Levante de chez Roca.

Modell Levante von Roca.

Roca Sureste Mod.

Mod. Sureste de chez Roca.

Modell Sureste von Roca.

Roca Genova Mod.

Mod. Genova de chez Roca.

Modell Genova von Roca.

Roca Karmine Mod.

Mod. Karmine de chez Roca.

Modell Karmine von Roca.

Roca Athica Mod.
with chromed legs.

*Mod. Athica sur pieds
chromés de chez Roca.*

Modell Athica
mit verchromten
Füßen von Roca.

Roca Mod.

Baignoire de chez Roca.

Badewanne von Roca.

Roca Miami Mod.

Mod. Miami de chez Roca.

Modell Miami von Roca.

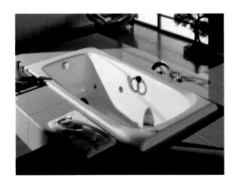

Roca Akira Mod.

Mod. Akira de chez Roca.

Modell Akira von Roca.

Roca Wing Mod.

Mod. Wing de chez Roca.

Modell Wing von Roca.

Roca Malibu Mod.

Mod. Malibu de chez Roca.

Modell Malibu von Roca.

Roca Continental Mod.

Mod. Continental de chez Roca.

Modell Continental von Roca.

Roca Haiti Mod.

Mod. Haiti de chez Roca.

Modell Haití von Roca.

Roca Swing Mod.

Mod. Swing de chez Roca.

Modell Swing von Roca.

Roca Malibu Mod.

Mod. Malibu de chez Roca.

Modell Malibú von Roca.

Roca Contesa Mod.

Baignoire de siège Contesa de chez Roca.

Modell Contesa von Roca.

Roca Duet Mod.

Mod. Duet de chez Roca.

Modell Duet von Roca.

Roca Holiday Mod.

Mini piscine Holiday de chez Roca.

Minischwimmbad Holiday von Roca.

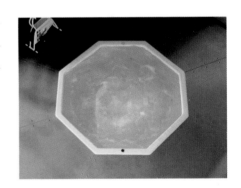

Roca Be Happy mini-pool.

Mini piscine Be Happy de chez Roca.

Minischwimmbad Be Happy von Roca.

Roca Swing Mod.

Mod. Swing de chez Roca.

Modell Swing von Roca.

Roca Haiti 2000 Mod.

Mod. Haiti 2000 de chez Roca.

Modell Haiti 2000 von Roca.

Roca Catamaran Mod.

Mod. Catamaran de chez Roca.

Modell Catamarán von Roca.

Roca Waitara Mod.

Mod. Waitara de chez Roca.

Modell Waitara von Roca.

Roca Qualia Mod.

Mod. Qualia de chez Roca.

Modell Qualia von Roca.

Roca Genova Mod.

Mod. Genova de chez Roca.

Modell Genova von Roca.

Roca Veranda Mod.

Mod. Veranda de chez Roca.

Modell Veranda von Roca.

Roca Levante Mod.

Mod. Levante de chez Roca.

Modell Levante von Roca.

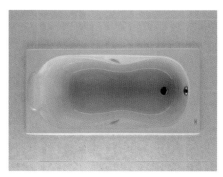

Roca Genova Mod.

Mod. Genova de chez Roca.

Modell Genova von Roca.

Roca Bali Mod.

Mod. Bali de chez Roca.

Modell Bali von Roca.

Roca Jamaica Mod.

Mod. Jamaica de chez Roca.

Modell Jamaica von Roca.

Roca Varadero Mod.

Mod. Varadero de chez Roca.

Modell Varadero von Roca.

Roca Duet Mod.

Mod. Duet de chez Roca.

Modell Duet von Roca.

Roca Veranda Mod.

Mod. Veranda de chez Roca.

Modell Veranda von Roca.

Hoesch oval bathtub.

Baignoire ovale indépendante de chez Hoesch.

Freistehende ovale Badewanne von Hoesch.

Hoesch oval bathtub with wall attachment.

Baignoire ovale adossée au mur de chez Hoesch.

Ovale Badewanne mit Wandanbindung von Hoesch.

Freestanding tub
with hand-held shower.

*Baignoire et douches séparées
du restant de la salle de bain.*

Badewanne und Dusche
in einem vom Badezimmer
abgetrennten Bereich.

Nineteenth-century style bathtub.

*Baignoire ancienne similaire
aux modèles utilisés au XIX ème siècle.*

Alte Badewanne stilgleich mit den im 19.
Jahrhundert gebräuchlichen Modellen.

An old cast iron bathtub
and set of porcelain-handled accessories.

*Ancienne baignoire en fonte restaurée et batterie
avec commandes en porcelaine qui remémorent les
salles de bain légendaires des balnéaires.*

Eine alte restaurierte GuBeissenbadewanne und
eine Mischbatterie mit Porzelangriffen evinnern
an die legendären Bäder der Kurorte.

Showers / *Les douches*
Duschen

Taking a shower is no longer a hygienic activity done in haste but one more occasion to enjoy the pleasure of something that is the equivalent of a physical exercise session. The new hydromassage or sauna cabins bring to the home the luxuries that until only a short time ago belonged to beauty centers, occupying the same space as a conventional shower. The advantages are to be found in their interior, in a whole hierarchy of controls for different types of water pressures and flows that massage different body parts until a sensation of general wellbeing has been achieved. The shower plates reduce their thickness through the use of highly resistant materials without any loss in all-important personal safety.

Prendre une douche n'est plus une action a réaliser à toute vitesse. Celle-ci est devenue une véritable partie de plaisir tout en réalisant l'équivalent à une session d' exercice physique. Les nouvelles cabines d'hydro massage ou de sauna ont apporté à nos foyers toutes sortes de soins qui était réservés auparavant aux salons de beauté tout en occupant le même espace qu'une douche conventionnelle. L'avantage se trouve à l'intérieur, car toute une hiérarchie de commandes permettent l'émission de différentes modalités de jets aquatiques qui massent le corps de tous les cotés pour atteindre une sensation de bien-être générale. Les plateaux de douche jouent à réduire leur épaisseur grâce à des matériaux très résistants qui ne nuisent absolument pas à la sécurité indispensable.

Sich zu duschen ist nicht mehr nur eine hygienische Aktivität, welche man schnellstmöglich hinter sich bringt, sondern eine weitere Gelegenheit sich den SpaB einer, mit einer physischen Leibesübung vergleichbaren Tätigkeit zu verschaffen. Die neuen Druckstrahlmassgekabinen und Saunen bringen Pflege nachhause, welche bis vor kurzem nur in Schönheitssalons zu finden war, und das bei einem Platzaufwand der einer konventionellen Dusche gleicht. Die Vorteile finden wir in ihrem Inneren, in einer Hirarchie von Steuerungen, die in verschiedenen Formen Wasser ausstrahlen, welches den Körper so lange hier und dort massiert, bis ein allgemeines Wohlbefinden erreicht wird. Die Duschwannen versuchen sich im Reduzieren ihrer Dicke durch sehr wiederstandsfähige Materialien, ohne dabei Abstriche in der unerlässlichen Sicherheit in Kauf zu nehmen.

Previous page:
Magma Network Mod.

Page précédente:
Mod. Network de chez Magma.

Auf der vorherigen Seite:
Modell Network von Magma.

Detail, Network plate edge.

Détail du rebord du plateau
de douche du mod. Network.

Detailansicht des Randes
der Wanne Network.

Roca Aquakit Comfort
hydromassage column.

*Colonne d'hydro massage
Aquakit Comfort
de chez Roca.*

Druckstrahlmassagesäule
Aquakit Comfort von Roca.

Detail, Aquakit column.

Détail de la colonne Aquakit.

Detailansicht der Säule Aquakit.

Roca Aquakit Plus Ducha
hydrosauna cabin.

*Cabine d'hydro sauna Aquakit
Plus Ducha de chez Roca.*

Hydrosaunakabine
Aquakit Plus Ducha von Roca.

Roca hydromassage
cabin.

*Cabine d'hydro
massage mod.
Aquatech
de chez Roca.*

Druckstrahlmassage
kabine Modell
Aquatech S von Roca.

Roca hydromassage
cabin.

*Cabine d'hydro massage
de chez Roca.*

Druckstrahlmassage
kabine von Roca.

Roca Aquatech Club
Mod. hydromassage
cabin.

*Cabine d'hydro
massage mod.
Aquatech Club
de chez Roca.*

Druckstrahlmassage
kabine Modell
Aquatech Club
von Roca.

Roca Paradise Mod.
hydromassage column
with screen plate.

*Porte vitrée Quartz pour
plateau de douche mod.
Paradise de chez Roca.*

Druckstrahlmassage
kabine Modell Aquatech
Club von Roca.

Roca MR quartz screen
plate corner-fitted
shower.

*Porte vitrée Quartz pour
plateau de douche mod.
Paradise de chez Roca.*

Quartzglaswand für
Duschwannen
Modell Paradise
von Roca.

Roca Aquakit Basic
hydromassage cabin.

*Cabine d'hydro massage
Aquakit Basic de chez Roca.*

Druckstrahlmassagekabine
Aquakit Basic von Roca.

Roca Aquakit Comfort
hydromassage column
for bathtubs.

*Colonne d'hydro massage
pour baignoire Aquakit Comfort
de chez Roca.*

Druckstrahlmassagesäule
für Badewannen Aquakit
Comfort von Roca.

Roca Aquakit Plus Vapor
Mod. cabin.

*Cabine mod. Aquakit Plus
Vapor de chez Roca.*

Massagekabine Modell
Aquakit Plus Vapor von Roca.

Roca Aquakit corner-fitted
hydromassage column.

*Colonne d'hydro massage en
angle Aquakit de chez Roca.*

Eckdruckstrahlmassagesäule
Aquakit von Roca.

Roca Supra L2 Mod. hydromassage screen.

Porte vitrée mod. Supra L2 de chez Roca.

Glaswand Modell Supra L2 von Roca.

Roca MR quartz screen plate
corner-fitted shower.

Porte vitrée Quartz MR de chez Roca.

Glaswand Quartz MR von Roca.

Roca Notario Mod.
shower plate.

Plateau de douche mod.
Notario de chez Roca.

Duschwanne
Modell Notario von Roca.

Roca Flamingo Mod.
ultra-thin shower plate.

Mod. extra Flamingo plat
de chez Roca.

Extraflache Duschwanne
Modell Flamingo von Roca.

Roca Opening Mod.
ultra-thin shower plate.

*Plateau de douche extra plat
mod. Opening de chez Roca.*

Extraflache Duschwanne
Modell Opening von Roca.

Roca Veranda Mod.
ultra-thin shower plate.

*Plateau de douche extra plat
mod. Veranda de chez Roca.*

Extraflache Duschwanne
Modell Veranda von Roca.

Lighting / *L'éclairage*
Beleuchtung

Bathroom lighting is designed to create a pleasant environment in the space, combining it with chosen spotlights in the area of the mirror. These spots must be precise but at the same time embellishing elements. Appliqués are the most common solution in the bathroom, sometimes in the form of halogen lamps, others in the form of conventional spotlights. The trend permits the incorporation of crazes inherited from *lo stile Liberty* passed through the sieve of today's new materials. Deluxe artisanship with the author's seal of approval.

Les lumières dans les salles de bain ont la mission de créer une ambiance agréable en combinaison avec quelques points lumineux précis situés près du miroir. Celles-ci doivent être à la fois belles et précises. Les appliques sont la solution la plus courante pour les salles de bain, parfois sous forme d'halogènes, d'autres sous forme de spots conventionnels. Il est aussi possible de se permettre quelques « folies » héritées du style Liberty passé par le tamis de nouveaux matériaux. Un artisanat de luxe avec la marque de l'auteur.

Die Lichtquellen des Badezimmers werden entworfen um eine angenehme Stimmung beim Aufenthalt kombiniert mit konkreten Lichtpunkten in Spiegelnähe zu schaffen. Diese müssen einerseits genau aber andererseits auch verschönernd sein. Wandleuchten sind die gebräuchlichste Lösung für das Badezimmer, teilweise als Halogenlampen und manchmal auch als konventionelle Scheinwerfer. Die Zeit erlaubt die Aufnahme von "Verücktheiten", vererbt aus dem Libertystil und ausgesiebt mit neuen Materialien. Ein Luxuskunsthandwerk mit dem Stempel des Autors.

Previous page:
Tulli Quadri 1 Mod.

Page précédente:
Mod. Quadri de chez Tulli.

Auf der vorherigen Seite:
Modell Quadri von Tulli.

Teo-Gaia/Elledue Ab Mod.
accent lamp.

Appliques mod. Ab de Teo-Gaia
de chez Elledue.

Wandleuchte Modell Ab
von Teo-Gaia/Elledue.

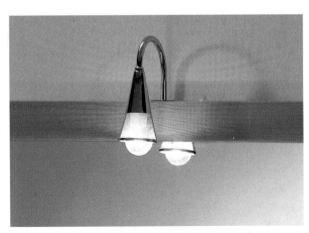

Roca Dicros I
accent lamps.

*Appliques Dicros
I de chez Roca.*

Wandleuchten
Dicros I von Roca.

Roca Veranda
accent lamps.

*Appliques
Veranda de chez
Roca.*

Wandleuchten
Veranda von Roca.

Roca Delta accent lamps.

*Applique au mur Delta
de chez Roca.*

Wandleuchte Delta, von Roca.

Roca focus.

Spot de chez Roca.

Scheinwerfer von Roca.

Roca focus.

Spot de chez Roca.

Scheinwerfer von Roca.

Elledue downlighting accent
lamps with glass screen.

*Lampe avec abat-jour
en verre de chez Elledue.*

Lampen mit Schirm
aus Glas von Elledue.

Detail, Elledue
downlighting lamp.

*Détail d'une lampe
de chez Elledue.*

Detailansicht einer
Elleduelampe.

Elledue downlighting accent
lamps with glass screen.

*Applique de coiffeuse
de chez Elledue.*

Wandleuchte für Toilettentisch
von Elledue.

Alchemy Lava Bath Roll Mod.

Mod. Lava Bath Roll de chez Alchemy.

Modell Lava Bath Roll von Alchemy.

Alchemy Lava V-Sconce Mod.

Mod. Lava V-Sconce de chez Alchemy.

Modell Lava V-Sconce von Alchemy.

Alchemy Fallen Leaves Mod.

Mod. Fallen Leaves de chez Alchemy.

Modell Fallen Leaves von Alchemy.

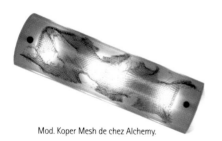

Mod. Koper Mesh de chez Alchemy.

Mod. Koper Mesh di Alchemy.

Modell Koper Mesh von Alchemy.

Alchemy Twilight Glass Mod.

Mod. Twilight Glass Cienaga de chez Alchemy.

Modell Twilight Glass von Alchemy.

Alchemy Fallen Leaves Pendant Mod.

Mod. Fallen Leaves Pendant de chez Alchemy.

Modell Fallen Leaves Pendant von Alchemy.

Alchemy Tribe Torciere Mod.

Mod. Tribe Torcière de chez Alchemy.

Modell Tribe Torciere von Alchemy.

Alchemy Copper Mesh Pendant Mod.

Mod. Copper Mesh Pendant de chez Alchemy.

Modell Copper Mesh Pendant von Alchemy.

Mod. Lava Cienaga Pendant de Alchemy.

Mod. Lava Cienega Pendant de chez Alchemy.

Modell Lava Cienega Pendant von Alchemy.

Alchemy MacMurphy Mod.

Mod. MacMurphy de chez Alchemy.

Modell MacMurphy von Alchemy.

Copat Zodiaco vanity lights.

*Spots de coiffeuse série Zodiaco
de chez Copat.*

Toilettentischbeleuchtung
Serie Zodiaco von Copat.

Detail, Copat vanity lights.

Détail des spots de chez Copat.

Detailansicht der
Beleuchtung von Copat.

Villeroy Nagano 2 Mod.

Mod. Nagano 2 de chez Villeroy.

Modell Nagano 2 von Villeroy.